BOOKISH
BROADS

For Liam and Maggie
My ultimate act of creativity;
you inspire me every day

Editors: Laura Dozier and Shannon Kelly
Designers: Diane Shaw and Jenice Kim
Production Manager: Kathleen Gaffney

Library of Congress Control Number: 2020931083

ISBN: 978-1-4197-4623-9
eISBN: 978-1-68335-955-5

Printed and bound in the United States
10 9 8 7 6 5 4 3 2 1

Abrams books are available at special discounts when purchased
in quantity for premiums and promotions as well as fundraising or
educational use. Special editions can also be created to specification. For
details, contact specialsales@abramsbooks.com or the address below.

ABRAMS The Art of Books
195 Broadway, New York, NY 10007
abramsbooks.com

BOOKISH BROADS

WOMEN WHO WROTE THEMSELVES INTO HISTORY

LAUREN MARINO
Illustrations by Alexandra Kilburn

ABRAMS IMAGE, NEW YORK

CONTENTS

INTRODUCTION

I am here to publicly confess that I am an addict—a book addict. I'm so hooked that I logged a super-geeky one hundred books during the summer between sixth and seventh grades. My reward (other than getting to constantly have my nose in a book) was a green T-shirt featuring a crazed monster and the declaration "Beware! I am a bibliomaniac!" I still have that T-shirt in a wardrobe in my childhood bedroom, and sometimes when I go visit my parents, I take it out and put it on—just in case anyone has forgotten who they are dealing with.

My bookworm ways have served me well as an English lit major, a professional book editor, and a published writer. Which is to say that in writing this book, it has been an absolute treat for me to delve deeply into the lives and work of the women I read growing up, those I've admired as an adult, and those whom I am—in my advanced stage of bibliomania—just now discovering. I am the girl who used to spend all day Saturday at the library on the floor in the stacks going further and further down the rabbit hole of research for a paper. And while I didn't enter academia (the siren song of New York book publishing lured me away), I maintained my love of digging deep into a subject, and, in this case, the subject—the many brave, brilliant, and downright amazing female storytellers—resonated with me so strongly that I was compelled to learn and explore further, in order to share this story with others.

Women have experienced restricted access to education throughout most of history—and, as we know too well (thank you, Malala), they still do in many parts of the world. I wanted to tell the stories behind the storytellers and explore the obstacles they had to overcome to become writers and create the lasting works that they did. And, by the way, if you look at the works of the women featured in this book chronologically, you'll see nothing less than a literary history of the female experience over the past thousand years.

What I discovered while writing this book is how much the greatest female writers have in common. They all loved books from a young age, and most started writing as soon as they could read. They were independent-minded and intelligent, and many were self-educated—a common characteristic all the way into the twentieth century. They had to somehow secure access, through fate or perseverance, not only to books but to the organizations—and publishers—that supported literature. And many of them used their minds and writing instruments—fountain pens, brushes, pencils, or computers—to make a case for educational and legal rights for women.

Most of these bookish broads also had to face vocal critics, who typically didn't have a lot of subtlety when it came to expressing their disdain. *Stick to your knitting. You have no talent. It isn't feminine; it's even downright immoral for a woman to publish.* If, as writer Lisa Kleypas said, a well-read woman is a dangerous creature, then what, pray tell, does that make a woman writer?

In a world where they had no voice, these women created one. Because, as we are still learning today, having a voice is how you get power. And through power, one can right the wrongs of the world. Or at least try to.

I had to make some tough choices about whom to include in this book, and sometimes I selfishly chose the women whose writing I personally loved or who I thought were particularly interesting or groundbreaking in some way. I couldn't even begin to delve into the poets, which is a book unto itself. Don't be mad if your favorite author isn't in here. I simply ran out of space and time. There are so many talented and renowned writers that I couldn't possibly fit them all in these pages, and I'm as sorry about that as you are.

There are other factors that limit the women who appear in this collection. Many of the most renowned international literary ladies are only beginning to be translated into English, and if their work is not available in English, I can't read them. And when slavery was in effect, black women in the United States were forbidden from learning to read or write, so earlier writing by them is scarce. This, and the countless untold stories and talented women whose voices have been lost to readers through oppression or prejudice, is a subject that deserves an entire book of its own.

This book isn't meant to be encyclopedic or exhaustive; it's meant to celebrate a selection of women who took up their pens, who were compelled to express themselves and comment on what they saw as flaws in society or on frustrations in their own lives that might resonate with other women. My hope in telling their stories is that you will be inspired to read some of their work and to understand the amazing legacy of female writers that is too often underappreciated. Still.

To this end, as a part of each profile, I have included some recommendations for further reading, if you are looking to explore the works of any of the women here in more detail. These recommendations are not comprehensive, but they offer a starting point.

This is a book for all book lovers, for readers but also for writers and aspiring writers of all ages and backgrounds. Anyone who has ever poured their heart and soul onto paper and then pared it down, reworked it, and revised it, trying to make it sing, knows the difficulty and self-doubt involved in putting ideas into words. To do all of that, despite the harsh criticism, overt discrimination, and limited access to education, resources, and fair pay that most of these women faced—well, it just goes to show how determined these writers were.

All of the unconventional rabble-rousers featured in the pages that follow wrote themselves into history. They were ahead of their time, and they didn't let their fear get the best of them. They were able to express their vision so well that their works continue to make an impact today, and with this book, I hope to do my part in honoring their legacy and helping a new generation of readers and writers find inspiration and hope in their incredible stories.

Happy reading!

I have a theory of my own about what the art of the novel is, and how it came into being . . . it happens because the storyteller's own experience . . . has moved him to an emotion so passionate that he can no longer keep it shut up in his heart.

—**LADY MURASAKI SHIKIBU**

MURASAKI SHIKIBU

978–1025

---◆◆◆◆---

What is widely considered the first novel ever written, the legacy of which is still a cultural and literary force today, was written in Japan in the eleventh century by a woman. The legend goes that Lady Murasaki was inspired to write *The Tale of Genji* on a religious retreat while gazing at the full moon. She took up her inkstone and writing brushes and wrote a sweeping tale that would enchant readers for centuries to come.

In this epic romance, coming in at a cool 1,300 pages, made up of fifty-four chapters and more than four hundred characters, it is the men who prance around like peacocks at the Imperial Court while women are subdued and sequestered. Prince Genji, the "Shining Prince," is perfumed, beautiful, a master of poetry and seduction, in an effete culture devoted to aesthetic refinement where beauty and style are considered karmic virtues. Despite the influence of Buddhism in Heian Japan (794–1185), appearance, elegant handwriting, and the ability to write good poetry were more important than any moral principles. Superficial? Perhaps, but enter Murasaki to chronicle this time period and move the arts forward, establishing a new, fundamental literary genre.

The Tale of Genji's keen observations of the decadent, opulent, and promiscuous life at court and the tangled-up emotions of love, lust, jealousy, and heartbreak could be written only by someone in the court but not *of* the court. This female courtier, whose actual name is not known, came to be known as Lady Murasaki, so called after the great, tragic lover of Genji, a vain Don Juan whose high birth allowed him to have many wives and concubines. Her premature death halfway through the novel devastates Genji—and the reader.

What is known of the author is that she was born to a provincial governor and scholar, a lower-ranking member of the Fujiwara clan, whose men often held high positions in the imperial government. Her mother died shortly after she was born. She is said to have learned Chinese by hiding behind the door while her father taught her brother. Her knowledge of literary Chinese was considered improper for an aristocratic lady at that time, because it was the official written language of government, also known as "men's letters." Women wrote "kana," or "women's hand," which was colloquial Japanese.

In Heian culture, females were valued for their skill in poetry, calligraphy, and the ability to make a good marriage. After her much older husband died, Murasaki was invited to the Empress Shōshi's court, probably because of her writing prowess. She wrote *Genji* as a serialized novel, reading it out loud at court. At the time, ink and paper were extremely scarce, yet her masterpiece was copied by hand and circulated widely enough to become an almost immediate sensation.

At court, communication was conducted in brief poems, or *waka*, composed at writing boxes, which were a sort of "rap battle" of poetry exchanges. *Genji* is influenced by this practice, containing a combination of poetry, lyrical prose, internal dialogue, and exposition that describes the intricate ceremonies, rivalries, jealousies, gossip, social climbing, and amorous conquests of day-to-day life at court. Murasaki also lushly details perfume making, costumes, furnishings, and even superstitions. For example, it was believed that women had the ability to use their jealousy as a weapon against their rivals by invoking evil spirits. How much fun would that be?

Murasaki's psychological insights were astute. She wryly examines female emotions and relationships between men and women in a polyamorous society where marriage and politics went hand in hand. Her themes included reincarnation, Buddhist symbols, the fragile nature, folly, and sorrow of our brief lives, and the futility of the human condition. She not only revealed the mores and culture of a fascinating society but also helped popularize Japanese prose, despite the fact that *The Tale of Genji* was written from a woman's point of view and told stories that were considered less serious and therefore beneath the interest of men.

As a result, women created the first indigenous Japanese literature. She created a literary aesthetic and standard that have been widely imitated and revered as proper, aristocratic Japanese. The universal themes and rich textures of this brilliant multigenerational saga still capture readers' emotions today.

FURTHER READING

The Tale of Genji, by Murasaki Shikibu, translated by Arthur Waley

The Tale of Murasaki: A Novel, by Liza Dalby (a transporting and historically accurate novel of Murasaki's life that intersperses her poetry and dialogue with the story)

MEDIEVAL MYSTICS

In the Middle Ages in Europe, most women were not educated or even literate (most men weren't literate either). Books were scarce, and women, as veritable baby-making machines, often experienced lives that were "nasty, brutish, and short." Women faced near constant pregnancy and childbirth starting at puberty. There's a reason it was called the Dark Ages! For the intellectually or creatively inclined, becoming a nun was the best bet to escape this fate, have some peace and quiet, and stimulate the mind. While convents may seem like a restrictive environment to us, many of the first female scholars and writers found freedom from marriage and the dangerous business of childbirth within their walls. Here, women could find learning, inspiration, and a room—actually a small rectangular stone cell—of their own.

HILDEGARD VON BINGEN
1098–1179

◆◆◆

At a time when Church teachings forbade women to write or speak in public, Hildegard heard an inner voice—or, as she believed, the voice of God—compelling her to put her thoughts and visions down on paper (in her case, a wax tablet, the writing on which was then transferred to parchment by a scribe).

We cannot live in a world that is not our own, in a world that is interpreted for us by others. An interpreted world is not a home. Part of the terror is to take back our own listening, to use our own voice, to see our own light.

———

Hildegard started receiving divine visions as early as age five and became a

nun at fourteen and eventually a Benedictine abbess. She was told to "say and write all that you see and hear." In her forties, she started recording her visions, and although she most likely dictated it, her *Scivias* (*Know the Ways*) is an original, autobiographical work of her connection to the divine. She knew Latin, and, despite her inability to write in her native German, she was learned and knew classical literature, the Scriptures, and philosophy. She also wrote on the subjects of science, medicine, natural history, theology, and music. Considered a prophetess, she was consulted and revered by everyone from the pope and kings to common laborers. Becoming a medieval celebrity was no small accomplishment, and Hildegard did it with her words.

JULIAN OF NORWICH
1342–1416

◆◆◆

Centuries before flower power or a mainstream understanding that "God is Love," Julian of Norwich claimed in her *Revelations of Divine Love in Sixteen Showings*, "'Would you learn to see clearly your Lord's meaning in this thing? Learn it well: Love was his meaning. Who showed it to you? Love . . . Why did he show it to you? For Love' . . . Thus I was taught that Love was our Lord's meaning."

When Julian was thirty, she became ill and almost died. A priest showed her an image of Christ on the cross, and she recovered, receiving sixteen visions, or revelations, that became the subject of her most famous work. In *Revelations*, she expresses her fear of death and the solace she found: "Just as our contrariness here on earth brings us pain, shame and sorrow, so grace brings us surpassing comfort, glory, and bliss."

Just because I am a woman, must I therefore believe that I must not tell you about the goodness of God, when I saw at the same time both his goodness and his wish that it should be known?

———

Julian had little to no formal education and called herself "unlettered," yet her work, written with vivid and sophisticated imagery, shows imagination, intellect, and a deep understanding of theology. Her metaphysical insights remain as appealing and comforting today as when they were written and have inspired writers as diverse as Iris Murdoch and T. S. Eliot. Not bad for a self-proclaimed "simple creature" sequestered in a stone cell.

SAINT TERESA OF ÁVILA
1515–1582

◆◆◆

Born during the Spanish Inquisition, Saint Teresa of Ávila was one of the great Christian mystics. She wrote, "There are more tears shed over answered prayers than over unanswered prayers," which, incidentally, Truman Capote used as the epigraph and title for his last, posthumously published novel, *Answered Prayers*.

But always when I was without a book, my soul at once became disturbed, and my thoughts wandered.

When Teresa was sixteen her father sent her to a convent to gain an education and possibly to escape disgrace for indiscretions with a suitor. Suffering from malaria, she began to experience intense visions she called "devotions of ecstasy" that helped her transcend her pain.

At forty, Teresa read Saint Augustine's *Confessions*, which inspired her to start traveling around Spain, founding several new convents focusing on the traditional values of poverty and simplicity. The patriarchal Church did not appreciate her work and called her "a restless disobedient gadabout who has gone about teaching as though she were a professor." Through many illnesses and near-constant criticism, she managed to maintain a sense of humor, optimism, and strength, and she expressed these in her work.

Teresa wrote several volumes of poetry and spiritual instructions. She is best known for her autobiography, *The Book of Her Life*, in which she describes the self-doubts, self-incriminations, and illnesses that led to her spiritual transformation. Her work has been translated into several languages, reaching a large audience all over the world, and in 1970 she was the first woman honored with the title Doctor of the Church. Her wisdom is still read by those seeking self-improvement and inspiration.

SAINT CATHERINE OF SIENA
1347–1380

◆◆◆

A spiritual activist, Catherine of Siena is known mostly for her 385 surviving letters and a number of other texts, the most significant being what she referred to as her *Dialogue*, 167 chapters of transcribed conversations between herself and God. It was dictated while she was in a state of ecstasy and had powerful influence over the politics and religious life of her time. It is considered a literary masterpiece and one of the first examples of enduring Italian literature.

Catherine was born to a poor wool dyer, the twenty-fourth of twenty-five children, and had her first vision of Christ when she was six. Can you blame her for, after her mother's constant childbearing, taking a vow of chastity at age seven?

> We've had enough exhortations to be silent. Cry out with a thousand tongues—I see the world is rotten because of silence.

She didn't learn to read or write until later in her life, calling upon her community of educated women— namely other nuns—to teach her. Latin was the language of men, the Church, the learned, and the elite, so she chose to write in vernacular Italian, in order to reach the widest possible audience, including women. She began corresponding with people from all walks of life around Italy, using rich metaphors and imagery to communicate with peasants, prisoners, royalty, and even the pope.

The male power structure didn't like her meddling in their affairs, complaining, "She's a woman. Why doesn't she stay in her cell?" But in her letters, she deployed a sense of humor, a deep spiritual wisdom, and a religious deference and charm that were extremely persuasive. She wrote several influential letters to Pope Gregory XI, cheekily addressing him as "Babbo," Italian for "Daddy," instead of "His Holiness," even when chiding him. Now that takes guts!

Her prayers and devotion led to several incidents that can only be called miracles (during the scourge of the Black Death, her touch was thought to heal people). She lived what she wrote, particularly, "Be who God meant you to be and you will set the world on fire." She spoke truth to power and used her words to negotiate for peace during difficult political times, becoming an influential public figure and humanitarian.

SECULAR SCRIBES

While the medieval mystics used divine intervention as their reason for writing, women at court had their high birth to thank for an education. In other words, you had to either become a nun or be lucky enough to be extremely rich and the daughter of a powerful man in order to read and write in those early times. The secular writers wrote about more earthy matters, namely about love between men and women and all its complications. The two best-known female writers of this time took chivalric romances, where men pined for passive female objects of desire, and turned them on their head. They wrote of courtly love from a woman's perspective and in a woman's voice, championing their gender and showing they could be as ribald and witty as their male counterparts.

MARIE DE FRANCE
Twelfth Century

We know very little about one of the first recorded female authors in Europe, other than what she wrote as an epilogue to one of her works: "Marie is my name and I am from France." She was one of the first women to write in vernacular French, and her witty and playful short narrative romances in verse, called *The Lais of Marie de France*, were wildly popular.

Marie was well educated and wrote in Latin, French, and English, and while she was probably born in Normandy, most of her manuscripts were discovered in England. She also referenced Greek mythology and elements of the supernatural in her storytelling. Her subject matter implies she was probably not a nun, and her poems caused a bit of a commotion when they were circulated—or sang and recited—because they went against the Church's teachings regarding virginity and the sanctity of marriage. She flipped the script, writing in a woman's voice where the damsel had agency and sometimes rescued the knight in distress.

Most of us know some of Aesop's fables, like "The Tortoise and the Hare," but Marie wrote her own original short tales based on the fables—102 in all—some of which were definitely not for children. Yes, they taught moral lessons,

> He to whom God has given knowledge And the gift of speaking eloquently Must not keep silent or conceal the gift But he must willingly display it

———

and some involved tales of animals who had human-like characteristics, such as "The Wolf and the Lamb," where a naive lamb becomes the wolf's dinner. But she also wrote longer fables involving humans, such as "About a Woman and Her Paramour" and "Another Story of a Woman and Her Paramour" (clearly, paramours were crowd pleasers), in which betrayal, treachery, shame, murder, and rape were all written into hilarious romps.

Yeah, she was clearly not a nun.

CHRISTINE DE PIZAN
1364–1430

✦✦✦

Christine de Pizan's father was the court astrologer for Charles V, a king known for his library. She was encouraged to explore it, and there, she educated herself, reading history, the work of the ancients, philosophy, and the sciences. She was married at fifteen to the court secretary and had a happy marriage, but when both her father and her husband died from the plague, Christine was left to care for her three children, mother, and niece. Without legal rights or knowledge of their husband's financial affairs, widows were often left destitute. For thirteen years Christine had to fight corrupt government officials who tried to cheat her out of money due to her husband, and she began writing romantic ballads, partially to deal with her grief and outrage over the injustice, but also to gain patronage. Her first work, *One Hundred Ballads*, was presented at court, and the aristocracy loved the novelty of a woman writing love poetry and began sponsoring her so she could earn her living.

She wrote typical courtly love poems, full of brave knights and fair damsels, in which the disenchanted narrator mourns the loss of a lover.

> Should I also tell you whether a woman's nature is clever and quick enough to learn speculative sciences as well as to discover them? I assure you that women are equally well-suited and skilled to carry them out and to put them to sophisticated use once they have learned them.

———

Writing from a female point of view, she satirized misogyny and showed how her narrator overcame troubles and heartbreak through resolve and intelligence. In addition to her poetry, she wrote novels, a biography, and an autobiography, as well as literary, political, and religious commentary—all highly unusual for a woman at that time.

Her best-known works are *The Book of the City of Ladies* and *The Treasure of the City of the Ladies* (or *The Book of the Three Virtues*). In these, Reason, Justice, and Rectitude build a city that allows women to have the same rights as men in order to take care of themselves, their homes, and families. She also mentions and honors virtuous women throughout history and places their accomplishments on the same level as those of men.

Christine was so successful that even in her own lifetime her work was translated into other languages, and after her death her books stayed in print and were published alongside and held in equal esteem with Chaucer's *Canterbury Tales*, Sir Thomas Malory's *Le Morte d'Arthur* (an early telling of King Arthur tales), and Aesop's fables.

SHAKESPEARE'S SISTERS

In *A Room of One's Own*, Virginia Woolf imagines that William Shakespeare had an equally talented and gifted sister—she calls her Judith—and shows how, as a woman, she would have been denied the same opportunities as her brother. The three women discussed in this section are, in a sense, three real-life Judiths. They were Shakespeare's peers but have been overlooked by many a history book. They had a level of privilege unknown to most women of their time, given their education and fame as femme savants, and many of the dramatic details of their colorful and intertwining lives did, indeed, make it into Shakespeare's plays and sonnets. They lived, however, at a time when a woman in the public eye, for her writing or any other cause, would be considered compromised and therefore subjected to sexist insults. While scholars disagree on whether these women actually wrote any of Shakespeare's works, they were most definitely his muses—but they also deserve to be celebrated for their own accomplishments.

MARY SIDNEY HERBERT, COUNTESS OF PEMBROKE
1561–1621

◆◆◆

Brilliant, brash, born into wealth and privilege, Mary Sidney was a fiery redhead like her queen and well educated, studying Latin, French, Italian, and Greek, as well as the more feminine pursuits of lute playing, singing, and needlework. She also had an alchemy lab, was interested in spiritual magic, and invented a recipe for disappearing ink.

At fifteen, Sidney went to court and married one of the richest men in England, the Earl of Pembroke. She surrounded herself with talented and well-known artists, poets, and musicians. When her famous brother, Sir Philip Sidney, a poet, statesman, and national hero, died in battle, she jumped on the opportunity to take over and rewrite his unfinished works, adding her own spin.

She was quite a virtuoso and hid her literary ambitions behind faux humility and the confines of the roles and genres that were allowed for women in her time: eulogy, elegy, translations, dedications to patrons, and religious works. Her brazenness was in publishing all of her work under her own name, without apology, and deliberately establishing her reputation as a writer. It didn't hurt that she was also a powerful patron of the arts, influencing and gaining praise from some of the major writers of the day, including Edmund Spenser, Michael Drayton, and Ben Jonson.

Sidney was born and died within a couple of years of Shakespeare, and it is believed by an entire group of scholars that she was, in fact, the real writer behind his work. *Antony and Cleopatra* was definitely influenced by her *The Tragedie of Antonie*—which, by the way, was the first dramatic play to be written and published by a woman. Her work and that of the Wilton Circle, the literary salon she created, became

sources for Shakespeare's plays. It is widely believed that her post-marriage life—where she threw fabulous parties, danced, sang, shot pistols, smoked, gambled, and took up with her much younger doctor—inspired his sonnets. And the family drama and literary inclination seemed to be contagious: Her niece and goddaughter, Mary Wroth, bore two illegitimate children to Sidney's son and wrote about Sidney's love affair with her doctor in her pastoral drama *Love's Victory*.

LADY MARY WROTH
1587–1653

—◆◆◆—

L ady Mary Wroth, the niece of Mary Sidney, took her aunt's work a step further, writing secular love poetry and romances, owning genres traditionally associated only with men. Her major work of prose fiction, *The Countess of Montgomery's Urania*, had thinly disguised allusions to the dramatics of her own love life and the scandals at court. Its publication caused quite a ruckus— the stories and details were just a little too specific and familiar to those in her social circle, and so they lashed out at her publicly, calling her "wanton" and a "hermaphrodite."

Mary's unhappy arranged marriage to Sir Robert Wroth, who was once described as "the foulest Churle in the world; he hath only one vertu that he seldom cometh sober to bed," inspired much of her work. He was not interested in literature and had only one book, a treatise on mad dogs, dedicated to him. Enough said.

Her first poems circulated widely before they were published, and her sonnet sequence *Pamphilia to Amphilanthus* was influenced by her love affair with William Herbert, Mary Sidney's elder son, which began before—and continued after—they were both married to other people. Wroth and their children often lived in William's house, which was next to the theater where he was Shakespeare's patron.

She makes her bitterness regarding their romantic arrangement pretty clear in the twenty songs and eighty-three sonnets in which her narrator, the loyal Pamphilia, is constant in her love for Amphilanthus, despite his unfaithfulness.

In *The Countess of Montgomery's Urania*, she creates a fully realized female character who turns tradition on its head—much as Wroth did in her own life with her brave writing and unconventional love life. She also created complicated plots and subplots, revolving around more than three hundred characters, and explored the oppression women faced, particularly being forced into marriage and enduring psychological and physical abuse, while men could play with and "trade" women among one another at will.

Wroth was also a major contributor to what would become a new genre in literature—the roman à clef (think: *The Devil Wears Prada*), disguising autobiography and aspects of real life as fiction.

AEMILIA BASSANO LANYER
1569–1645

The daughter of a Venetian musician whose family were Marrano Jews passing as Protestants after the Inquisition, poet Aemilia Lanyer is a controversial figure. Many scholars believe that she not only was the Dark

Lady of Shakespeare's sonnets but also wrote much of his work.

She was the mistress of Henry Carey, Lord Hunsdon, who as a general and judge was also the patron of the Lord Chamberlain's Men, who performed Shakespeare's plays. Her *Salve Deus Rex Judaeorum* (1611) has been called the first book of poetry to be published by a woman in England.

Although upper-class writers preferred not to appear in print—and God knows they didn't need the money—as a member of the middle class, Lanyer found support through patronage, which was what made one a "professional" writer. In return for attention and financial support, the writer would sing their patron's praises in verse in dedications, often comparing them to classical historical characters of high virtue. Lanyer actively sought a group of women to support her and wrote eleven dedications shouting out their achievements. At the time this was a bold statement, in that she was publicly proclaiming herself not only a professional poet but also the first writer to dedicate work exclusively to female patrons.

She claimed to have been called by God to write, hiding some of her subversive themes inside seemingly religious works. She wrote *Salve Deus* under the guise of devotional religious poetry—although in reality, it was more of a defense of women's rights and virtues. It reimagines the Christ narrative solely from a female point of view. She presents Pontius Pilate's wife, who tries to dissuade her husband from crucifying Jesus, as virtuous and men as vain and egotistic. This was a pretty radical statement—I mean, she rewrote the story of Christ! From a female perspective. In 1,840 lines of highly accomplished iambic pentameter (the same form Shakespeare used).

Whether she *was* Shakespeare, collaborated with him, or merely inspired him, she was clearly groundbreaking and talented, which is enough for me.

Restoration-Era Rebel

APHRA BEHN

1640–1689

————◆◆◆◆————

All I ask, is the privilege for my masculine part the poet in
me. . . . If I must not, because of my sex, have this freedom . . .
I lay down my quill and you shall hear no more of me.

————

Aphra Behn was forgotten to history until Virginia Woolf wrote about her, famously saying, "All women together ought to let flowers fall upon the tomb of Aphra Behn, for it was she who earned them the right to speak their minds."

Behn's "scandalous" work marginalized her—readers confused her strong, female, first-person narratives with the writer herself, and so she was condemned for her "loose morals" and largely forgotten until feminist scholars rediscovered her in the 1970s. The fact is, outside of her writing, we know very little about her.

Her biographer Janet Todd wrote that Behn "has a lethal combination of obscurity, secrecy and staginess which makes her an uneasy fit for any narrative, speculative or factual. She is not so much a woman to be unmasked as an unending combination of masks."

What we do know is that in 1664 she started writing under the name Mrs. Behn, which may be attributed to a brief marriage that ended with her husband's death or the couple's separation. It was a time of civil war and upheaval in England, and she became involved with the court, reportedly spying for King Charles II when he was at war with the Netherlands. Her code name was Astrea, which she later repurposed as her pen name. Unfortunately, the king never paid her for her services and a warrant was issued for her arrest; some say she went to debtor's prison, having had to pawn her jewels and borrow money in order to survive overseas and return home.

Always a poet, she began writing plays as a way to earn money during the robust and libertine Restoration era, when theaters reopened after being shut down for eighteen years by the Puritans. She became one of the first female playwrights in

England to have her plays staged openly and was published at a time when women were also appearing as actresses for the first time (in Shakespeare's era, all of the female roles were played by boys). The public's enthusiasm for the theater after such a dry spell resulted in some over-the-top bawdiness and social satire. Restoration comedies are hilarious sexual farces with a lot of cuckoldry, chases around the bed, and lovers literally—and figuratively—hiding in the closet. Astrea dove right in alongside her male counterparts and became wildly popular and successful.

Her first several plays about arranged marriages, including *The Forc'd Marriage*, *The Amorous Prince*, and *The Rover*, were favorites of the king and court. On the one hand, they loved her work, but on the other they harshly criticized her. How dare she not only write, but be successful at it too. So they accused her of plagiarism and lewdness. But she persisted. She had to earn a living, after all.

Despite her many critics, she could write as well as—and often better than—any of her male peers, using the same traditional forms: pastoral, allegory, biblical allusions, courtly love, the couplet, and the ballad. She published nineteen plays and four novels, as well as novellas, short stories, and poetry, becoming a celebrity among the literati and the public. Her subject matter reflected her views and politics: women's lack of access to education, sexual freedom for both sexes, antiwar statements, social satire, and contemporary events. In the preface to her play *The Luckey Chance*, she wrote that criticism of her work would not exist were she not a woman.

Her most famous novel, *Oroonoko*, published a year before her death, was written as a first-person narrative from a female perspective and was groundbreaking in describing the injustices of the slave trade.

Despite the haters trying to keep her down, Behn's versatility and contributions to developing the female narrative voice and helping develop the English novel—as well as her influence on the female writers who came after her—have brought her back from the dead in recent years. All of her work has been republished for a contemporary audience that is just now discovering her in the twenty-first century.

FURTHER READING

Oroonoko, The Rover and Other Works, by Aphra Behn, introduction by Janet Todd (Penguin Classics Edition)

Aphra Behn: A Secret Life, by Janet Todd

The Tenth Muse

SOR JUANA INÉS DE LA CRUZ

1651–1695

————◆◆◆◆◆————

Juana Inés de Asbaje y Ramírez de Santillana was a beautiful, intelligent prodigy who so dazzled the Viceregal Court that she earned the nicknames "Phoenix of Mexico" and the "Tenth Muse." Apparently, her brilliance was such that nine muses were not enough. Born near Mexico City, she became one of the greatest Latin American poets, a self-educated scholar, and one of the first published feminist writers.

> Who has forbidden women to engage in private and individual studies? Have they not a rational soul as men do? . . . I have this inclination to study and if it is evil I am not the one who formed me thus—I was born with it and with it I shall die.

————

Despite the fact that girls were rarely educated, Sor Juana learned to read at age three, using books in her grandfather's library. At fifteen, she became a lady-in-waiting at court, where she entertained nobles with her poetry and plays and amazed university scholars who came and questioned her on subjects like mathematics, logic, physics, philosophy, literature, law, history, rhetoric, and music, of which she knew a great deal. She begged her parents to let her cut her hair and attend university dressed as a boy, but they laughed her off, so she moved to the Convent of San Geronimo, became a nun, and remained cloistered. She read tirelessly and wrote sonnets, romances, and dramatic and scholarly works that displayed an inventive wit and tremendous knowledge of both secular and nonsecular sources.

But she didn't live a traditional life of asceticism: Her cell was full of art, musical instruments, and four thousand (Four. Thousand.) books, and she had servants to care for her. She received the patronage of the viceroy of Mexico and developed an extremely close relationship with the vicerine, Countess Maria Luisa de Paredes, to whom she wrote love poetry. Her cell became a sort of salon, visited by intellectuals and nobility.

Sor Juana's two best-known poems are "Foolish Men" and "First Dream," which discuss the lack of logic in men's criticism of women and her almost spiritual quest for knowledge, respectively. Her plays featured strong, courageous, and intelligent women, and her love poems may be some of the first lesbian poetry in North America. One such poem admires the beauty of and expresses longing for a woman named Feliciana, who is believed to represent her patroness, the Countess.

It was extremely unusual for any writer at the time—male or female—to be published during their lifetime, but Sor Juana's collected works were printed and she also edited her own biography, which would be published after her death. Her popularity and fame brought criticism from the Church at a time when the Inquisition made attracting attention very dangerous. A bishop once published one of Sor Juana's critiques of a well-known Jesuit sermon under a female nun's pseudonym—Filotea de la Cruz—in a devious attempt to cause her trouble and perhaps invite persecution. Sor Juana was on to him, though, and published her response, her most famous work, *Respuesta a Sor Filotea de la Cruz*. In it, she wrote a classically structured rebuttal, defending women's rights to an education and claiming that knowledge of secular works was a necessary part of understanding theology.

She is considered an icon of the Spanish Golden Age and has been acknowledged in statuary; her former cloister is now a university bearing her name, University of the Cloister of Sor Juana de la Cruz; her face is etched in gold on the wall of honor in the Mexican Congress; and she graces the 200-peso banknote. Defiant, brilliant, a champion of the arts and sciences and women's rights, she is considered a Mexican national treasure.

◆ ◆ ◆ ◆ ◆ ◆ ◆ ◆ ◆ ◆ ◆ ◆ ◆ ◆

FURTHER READING

Sor Juana Inés de la Cruz: Selected Works, translated by Edith Grossman, introduction by Julia Alvarez

Sor Juana: Or, the Traps of Faith, by Octavio Paz, translated by Margaret Sayers Peden

◆ ◆ ◆ ◆ ◆ ◆ ◆ ◆ ◆ ◆ ◆ ◆ ◆ ◆

ON THE
DANGERS OF
ROMANTIC NOVELS

It was during the eighteenth century that the predecessors of Jane Austen began to chip away at the male-dominated world of literature in earnest. The times were a-changing, and established ideas of how young women should behave were starting to be challenged. The radical flight of fancy that marriage could perhaps involve love and companionship was beginning to take hold. Writers like Charlotte Lennox and Frances Burney began to write coming-of-age stories that tried to bring realism and a female perspective to the complicated notion of female virtue, which, heretofore, had been defined by men. They did this through sentimental and moralistic novels, which some called "absurd romantic fantasy."

Reader, a newly literate and hungry population devoured them. Circulation libraries sprang up, making books accessible and affordable to the masses for the first time, and romantic novels became the most popular genre. Reading was being done strictly for pleasure for the first time in history. This created panic among moralists and the upper classes. How dare the lower classes start reading books—for pleasure!—and trashy ones at that. Critics claimed that this early chick lit was dangerous to family life: Women were getting unrealistic romantic notions! They were raising daughters who would grow up looking for emotional and physical pleasure instead of being dutiful, subservient wives! An eighteenth-century bishop even claimed that reading novels would lead to prostitution, homosexuality, alcoholism, and more earthquakes.

For the patriarchy, the threat of widespread literacy among women can be a bitch.

CHARLOTTE LENNOX
1729–1804

◆◆◆

Charlotte Lennox appears in Richard Samuel's 1778 painting *Nine Living Muses of Great Britain* as part of a group of the most influential female intellectuals of that time, but she was no bluestocking. Over forty-three years, she published eighteen works, including six novels whose wit, satire, and independent female characters served as models for Jane Austen's novels, particularly *Northanger Abbey* and *Sense and Sensibility*.

The daughter of a soldier, Lennox entered an unhappy marriage with a man whose primary redeeming quality was that in working for the printer William Strahan, he exposed her to the London publishing market. She wasted no time taking advantage and published *Poems on Several Occasions* a month after her wedding.

By age thirty, she had created her own magazine, *The Lady's Museum*, which she called "A Course in Female Education," that included defenses for women's education as well as introductions to geography, history, biology, and philosophy. She helped pioneer the serialization of novels, by publishing a new chapter of her own works in progress in every issue.

Her first novel, *The Life of Harriot Stuart, Written by Herself*, was celebrated with a party thrown by none other than famous writer and wit Samuel Johnson—the man who literally wrote the first English dictionary.

Her best-known work was part imitation, part parody of Miguel de Cervantes's novel *Don Quixote*. Lennox's *The Female Quixote; or, The Adventures of Arabella* tells the story of an intelligent if naive heroine, whose entire understanding of life comes from French romances. It was a huge success that received critical praise from Henry Fielding, who called it "most extraordinary" and a "Work of true Humour." Samuel Johnson also lavished it with praise; it was the only novel he ever reviewed in his life.

She also helped elevate the status and legacy of William Shakespeare through her *Shakespeare Illustrated: Or, The novels and histories on which the plays of Shakespeare are founded*.

Her final work, *Euphemia*, was an epistolary novel drawing on her own life in which the heroine is taken to America by a dissolute husband who corrupts their child. In the novel, the husband gets his comeuppance and the heroine triumphs, taking control of the family money and seeing her beloved son returned to her. Sometimes we can only right the wrongs of real life through writing—and that was Lennox's sweet revenge.

FRANCES BURNEY
1752–1840

◆◆◆

Virginia Woolf called her the "mother of English fiction." A devoted and lifelong diarist, Frances Burney began chronicling her ideas about life as soon as she could read and write. She published her first novel, *Evelina*, at age twenty-six, albeit anonymously. Her considerable skill in writing an epistolary novel from a variety of characters' perspectives led her audience to assume it was written by a man. Naturally.

Burney created an entire new genre, the "comedy of manners," with realistic portrayals of women in contemporary situations. She went on to write *Cecilia*, a novel filled with sharp observations of the follies and foibles of society. It was a smash, selling extremely well and making her a literary celebrity.

Burney married a French émigré, and when his estate was confiscated, Fanny published her third novel, *Camilla*, and was able to purchase her husband's family home back.

At this time she was diagnosed with breast cancer and underwent an excruciating mastectomy—there was no anesthesia back then—which she painfully documented, the earliest such record of the procedure.

Burney became the first woman to make writing novels a respectable profession and laid the groundwork for female novelists to come. It is believed that Jane Austen borrowed a phrase from dialogue in *Cecilia* in which a Dr. Lyster states that "the whole of this unfortunate business has been the result of pride and prejudice."

Universally Acknowledged
to Have Modernized the Novel
JANE AUSTEN
1775–1817

———◆◆◆◆◆———

There's no question that the cult of Jane (Janeites, for those not in the know) is still going strong. More than two centuries after Austen's death, she is as popular as ever: Literary critics theorize about and analyze her, looking for a secret code that will reveal her political or feminist ideas, while fangirls escape into romantic fantasy. Her wild popularity spawned an entire subgenre of novel, the Regency romance, and provided fodder for a thousand—often inspired—knockoffs, whether populated by teenagers in 1995 Beverly Hills (*Clueless*) or muslin- and bonnet-wearing flesh eaters (*Pride and Prejudice and Zombies*).

> *The person, be it gentleman or lady, who has not pleasure in a good novel, must be intolerably stupid.*

———

The seventh of eight children, her father a solid middle-class vicar, Austen grew up in a rectory, attending school for only a few months over a two-year period. She was extremely close to her only sister, Cassandra, and they corresponded throughout their entire lives. It is through their letters that we know much of what we do of Austen, although many of the letters were burned by Cassandra after Austen died—we can only wonder what scandalous or juicy tidbits were in them!

Austen wrote about what she knew—the middle and upper classes of rural England and the importance of a beneficial marriage. Marriage was serious business in the early nineteenth century for both women and men; Austen satirized the social conventions and financial motivations for marriage and through her inde-

pendent heroines tried to create more liberal ideas of what a woman could achieve and aspire to. Though Austen entertained two or three flirtations, she herself chose not to marry. In one letter to Cassandra, she expressed distress at spoiled children, marriage, and childbearing ("Poor Woman! Can she be honestly breeding again?"). Other letters discuss her involvement with a young Irishman, Tom Lefroy, whose mother wouldn't let him marry her because she didn't have quite enough dosh to be posh (this story is the basis of the movie *Becoming Jane*, starring Anne Hathaway). She did accept a proposal from a neighbor that would have assured her financial stability, but, after sleeping on it, she woke up and exercised a woman's prerogative and changed her mind.

While she is widely thought to be the model for her most beloved character, Jane's life was a little more complicated than Lizzie Bennet's.

For her entire life, the world was at war, through the American Revolution, the French Revolution, and Napoleon's attempts at conquest. It was a volatile time, to say the least! Life was not all carriage rides and fancy-dress balls. Two of her brothers joined the navy, one joined the militia, and for a time she lived near the naval base in Southampton. She no doubt met her share of George Wickham–type scoundrels. Her brother Edward had been adopted and raised by their father's childless patrons, Thomas and Catherine Knight, and he inherited their estate at Chawton. When their father passed away, Edward invited his mother and sisters to live in a cottage on the grounds, which is where Austen wrote many of her greatest novels. So, yes, there was at least a fabulous country estate and soldiers running around to inspire her. There she established a writing routine while her sister and mother generously covered the housework for her.

Austen's writings, from as early as age eleven, including *History of England*, have some very funny mimicry involving religion and politics, and parodies that showed her deep knowledge of literary conventions and popular novels. Indeed, at school she read not only popular fiction but also *The Lady's Magazine*, with its fictional stories of its version of the modern woman.

Austen was the same age as Elizabeth Bennet (twenty-one) when she started writing *First Impressions*, which would eventually become *Pride and Prejudice*. She read her works in progress at home, and *P&P* was a family favorite. It was initially rejected by a publisher without having even been read. Austen put it aside and started working on *Elinor and Marianne*, which became *Sense and Sensibility*.

Since women couldn't legally sign contracts, the only way for her to eventually publish was through the involvement of one of her brothers. An acquaintance of her brother Henry, Thomas Egerton, agreed to print *Sense and Sensibility*. The initial print run was 750 copies—paper was expensive then, and paid for by the author—but they went back to press after the first run sold out. Austen didn't publish using her own name or an ambiguous male-sounding pseudonym. She maintained anonymity but made it clear that a woman had written the book by signing it "A Lady." She was an astute businesswoman in dealing with her publishers, and although she made only modest earnings from her books during her lifetime, she did have in mind a long-term plan to publish three more novels.

Austen published four novels while she was alive, two were published after her premature death from Addison's disease at age forty-one, and two more remained unfinished. It wasn't until the posthumous publication of her work and Henry's biographical notice that she was acknowledged as the author of all six. Her spirited and independent-minded heroines and their intelligence and wit have been role models of sorts for generations of young women.

And we'll always have Mr. Darcy.

FURTHER READING

Sense and Sensibility (1811)

Pride and Prejudice (1813)

Mansfield Park (1814)

Emma (1815)

Northanger Abbey (1818, posthumous)

Persuasion (1818, posthumous)

Jane Austen: A Life, by Claire Tomalin (one of many biographies but something of a fan favorite)

The Original Feminist

MARY WOLLSTONECRAFT

1759–1797

———◆◆◆◆———

Mary Shelley's mother was a groundbreaking advocate for change and had a deep influence on her, even though she died a few days after giving birth to her. While mother and daughter never knew each other, it is said that Shelley learned to read in part by tracing the letters on her mother Mary Wollstonecraft's gravestone—which somehow seems appropriate.

A humanist who believed in God-given rights and the pursuit of personal fulfillment for all people, Wollstonecraft authored many works, most notably the groundbreaking *A Vindication of the Rights of Woman*. In it she explored the need for women's education and equal status and rights in both public and domestic life, which made her famous overnight. In the 1947 anti-feminist work *Modern Woman: The Lost Sex*, the psychiatrist authors use Freudian analysis and Wollstonecraft as a case study to debunk feminism, calling her "an extreme neurotic of a compulsive type. . . . Out of her illness arose the ideology of feminism." So as of the mid-twentieth century, feminism was viewed as having been invented by Wollstonecraft but also as stemming from mental illness. Fascinating.

> I do not wish them [women] to have power
> over men; but over themselves.

———

A middle-class country girl whose abusive father drank away the family's wealth, Wollstonecraft received a haphazard education, mostly through her own reading, and led a turbulent life, realizing early on that living according to convention did not provide a woman with emotional or financial security. She struggled to support herself before moving to London and meeting up with a group of liberal

VINDICATION

OF THE

RIGHTS OF

WOMAN

intellectuals, writing for the reformist publisher Joseph Johnson's radical *Analytical Review*. She also originally sided with the revolutionaries in France, writing a pamphlet, *A Vindication of the Rights of Men*, endorsing their desire for *liberté* and *égalité*, which she believed belonged not just to the *fraternité* but also to the *sororité*. Unfortunately, as the revolutionaries became vicious with the guillotine, giving up many of their ideals in favor of revenge, an antirevolutionary sentiment developed in England that would cast a shadow over Wollstonecraft's work.

In her first book, *Thoughts on the Education of Daughters*, she argued for coeducation for boys and girls, specifically to give girls a "rational" education so that they could contribute more to society than doing needlepoint and bearing children. She also published *Mary: A Fiction* (an autobiographical novel), a children's book, and the travel narrative *Letters Written During a Short Residence in Sweden, Norway, and Denmark*, which through its sublime connection to nature helped initiate the Romantic movement in literature.

It was at a dinner party Samuel Johnson (that guy got around!) threw for Thomas Paine that Wollstonecraft met fellow writer and philosopher William Godwin. Despite both of them being against the institution of marriage, in which a woman lost her legal identity, she was soon pregnant and so they tied the knot. Ten days after the wedding, their daughter, Mary Wollstonecraft Godwin (later Shelley), was born, and Wollstonecraft died of septicemia from an infected placenta. Her daughter would come to know her mother through her writings.

After her death, her husband wrote a memoir of his life with her that was perhaps a little too frank, which led to his wife's condemnation in the eyes of the public (before marrying Godwin she had been involved with another man and had had an illegitimate child with him—Fanny Imlay; she refused last rights on her deathbed, proving herself not a Christian; and she attempted suicide, considered a mortal sin, twice after the father of her first child abandoned her). After this, her work was derided and mostly disappeared until the second half of the twentieth century, when she started to be fully read and understood as an important moral and political thinker who strove for social justice.

◆◆◆◆◆◆◆◆◆◆◆◆◆

FURTHER READING

A Vindication of the Rights of Woman, by Mary Wollstonecraft

◆◆◆◆◆◆◆◆◆◆◆◆◆

The Original Romantic Goth
MARY SHELLEY
1797–1851

———— ✦✦✦✦ ————

Beware, for I am fearless and therefore powerful.

————

The word that comes up again and again in Mary Shelley's life and writing is *chaos*. Given her mother's legacy, that's not surprising. In her own words, "Invention, it must be humbly admitted, does not consist in creating out of void, but out of chaos." She knows whereof she speaks: Her mother died within days of her birth, and she ran off with the married poet Percy Shelley in 1814 when she was just sixteen, resulting in estrangement from her beloved father and the suicide of Percy's pregnant wife. Shelley was constantly pregnant during their eight-year relationship, which resulted in several severe miscarriages and the deaths of three of her four children. Her half sister, Fanny, committed suicide in 1816, and Percy drowned in 1822, leaving her in poverty with their only remaining son.

Shelley received an unusual and rigorous, if informal, education. In addition to studying the classics, she had access to her father's extensive library and the many progressive ideas of the intellectuals who visited their home. She was raised as an anarchist, atheist, abolitionist, and freethinker, committed to economic justice and improving the role of women in society, which included the view that marriage was repressive (and if you've read up until this point, you'll recognize this was accurate). Despite this, she did marry Shelley and was devoted to him in life and in death, keeping what was believed to be his heart (they say she pulled it from his body at the gravesite) wrapped in one of his last poems in her desk, along with locks of hair from her dead children.

She famously began her masterpiece, *Frankenstein, or the Modern Prometheus*, at the urging of the notorious and, in the words of Lady Caroline Lamb, "mad, bad, and dangerous-to-know" literary lion Lord Byron. A small group of writers were stuck indoors at a large house in Lake Geneva during the stormy and wet summer after Mount Tambora erupted, throwing volcanic ash throughout Europe, creating crazy weather patterns and unusually low temperatures. Since the group was confined to the house for days at a time, they discussed current scientific theories, including whether or not electrical impulses could bring something dead back to life. Byron suggested they all write a ghost story to entertain themselves, and the story Shelley started that night eventually became the novel about Dr. Victor Franken-stein, a Swiss scientist who attempts to create life. The monster, in Victor's words, is "my own vampire, my own spirit let loose."

The book became an immediate worldwide phenomenon. People were initially convinced that it was her husband who had written the book; a young woman could never write something so dark, gruesome, and radical. She was eventually acknowl-edged as the true author, and the second edition was published with her name on it.

More than a spine-chilling horror story, *Frankenstein* wrestles with ideas such as the dangers of playing God and the nature and responsibility of creating, and the crucial role of women in society; and reflects on slavery and the hierarchies of race, the conflict between science and religion, the boundaries between life and death, and the tendency of man toward hubris through technology. (Of course, these themes are still relevant today, especially considering the power of Silicon Valley, the development of artificial intelligence, and the moral ambiguities of human cloning and gene editing.)

Dr. Frankenstein's creation kills everything that his creator loves and ultimately destroys him. And yet Shelley has great compassion for her "monster."

Mary also wrote seven other novels, including *Matilda*, a feminist critique of the patriarchy, and *The Last Man*, an apocalyptic novel that shows how little control humans have over history and improving their own condition. Her considerable literary output also included short stories, essays, magazine articles, biographies, and travelogues.

Mary extensively edited Percy's work and provided biographical references that helped create and preserve his legacy.

For anyone who thinks they know the story of Frankenstein because they've seen a movie or two, I dare you to read it. That the ideas in this book, which look at the very nature of life and death, were written by an eighteen-year-old woman in the early 1800s who had never been to school is astonishing.

FURTHER READING

Frankenstein, or the Modern Prometheus, by Mary Shelley

Romantic Outlaws: The Extraordinary Lives of Mary Wollstonecraft and Mary Shelley, by Charlotte Gordon

Masculin et Feminin

GEORGE SAND

(Amandine-Aurore-Lucile Dupin Dudevant)

1804–1876

———— ✦✦✦✦ ————

It makes sense that Amandine Dupin would use a male pseudonym, George Sand; she liked to provoke by dressing like a man on occasion and wanted a writing career that would give her the financial freedom of a man.

Born in Paris to a couple who got married just one month before she was born, Dupin was sent to the family estate in Berry, France, to be raised by her grandmother. Aurore, as she was called, learned the common skills of girls of her class: piano and harp, horseback riding (but she rode astride, like a boy, not sidesaddle), reading, poetry, philosophy, and the natural sciences. After a short stint being educated at a convent, she entertained the idea of becoming a nun. She eventually inherited the estate, married a baron, and had two children, but her alcoholic husband didn't respect her or her intelligence. She left him and the children, allowing him to keep the estate while she received an annual allowance. This gave her the freedom she craved.

> The world will know and understand me someday.
> But if that day does not arrive, it does not greatly matter.
> I shall have opened the way for other women.

————

She moved to Paris and started wearing men's clothing and hats, despite it being illegal for a woman to do so without a permit, in order to gain access to social settings where women weren't allowed (museums, libraries, literary clubs, and the pit of the theater, just to name a few). She smoked cigars in public, was politically

active, and preached free love, having had several love affairs with, among others, composers Franz Liszt and Frederic Chopin, as well as one with a woman. The poet Charles Baudelaire was not a fan of her unfeminine behavior and called her "stupid, heavy, and garrulous" and said, "The fact that there are men who could become enamoured of this slut is indeed proof of the abasement of the men of this generation." His fat- and slut-shaming did not prevent her, or her writing, from being held in high esteem by her male peers, including Dostoevsky, Proust, and Balzac.

She hung out with the artistic and intellectual elite and wrote for *Le Figaro* and other publications, working as co-editor of *Revue indépendante*, a Symbolist journal. She wrote about and advocated for the working class and women. She even became involved in politics, unheard-of for women, when she started her own Socialist newspaper.

Her first novel, *Rose et Blanche*, was co-written with one of her lovers under the pseudonym Jules Sand. After they broke up, she wrote her most enduring novel, *Indiana*, which was the first time she wrote under the name George Sand. Her protagonist is a young woman who tries to assert her independence by running away from her abusive husband. In it she explicitly calls marriage a form of slavery, which didn't go over so well, especially coming from the pen of an aristocratic woman.

Prolific in addition to scandalous, she went on to write more than seventy novels, twenty-four plays, ten volumes of autobiography, essays, literary criticism, political statements, and forty thousand letters. She would say, "Art for art's sake is an empty phrase. Art for the sake of truth, art for the sake of the good and the beautiful, that is the faith I am searching for."

In her life and in her work, she challenged the restrictions on women's freedoms and was steadfast in expressing her progressive views. She was truly ahead of her time, prompting the Russian novelist Ivan Turgenev to say of her, "What a brave man she was, and what a good woman." Her bravery and deliberate intentions helped pave the way to women finally becoming respected as serious writers in their own lifetime.

FURTHER READING

Indiana (1832)

Mauprat (1837)

La Mare au Diable (1846)

Story of My Life: The Autobiography of George Sand, translation coordinated by Thelma Jurgrau (1991, first published in 1854)

Not a Silly Novelist

GEORGE ELIOT

(Mary Ann Evans)

1819–1880

❖❖❖❖

You must not be ashamed of your work, and think it would be more honorable to you to be doing something else. You must have a pride in your own work and in learning to do it well.

George Eliot wrote *Middlemarch*, considered one of the greatest English novels of all time, under a male pseudonym. She also wrote a scathing essay called "Silly Novels by Lady Novelists," criticizing her female peers for writing romances with shallow plots and characters; she was one of the first to reject the unrealistic Cinderella story trope where a beautiful, intelligent woman of great virtue falls madly in love, gets married, and lives happily ever after. "Silly Novels" can be viewed as a treatise on what fiction shouldn't do, namely, be riddled with clichés and mistake "vagueness for depth, bombast for eloquence, and affectation for originality."

Eliot was born Mary Ann Evans in Warwickshire, England, on the sprawling grounds of Arbury Hall and Estate, which her father managed. Her upbringing was the inspiration for many of her novels, in which she wrote vividly about the landscape and real-to-life rural characters. She went to boarding school from age five until her mother's death, after which, at seventeen, she returned home to run the household. Eliot started writing for *The Westminster Review* in 1851, eventually becoming its editor—albeit anonymously, since, in the words of biographer Brenda Maddox, "a female editor was as unheard of as a female surgeon."

A devout Christian in her youth, Eliot began to question her religious beliefs as an adult. She began translating controversial works by German freethinkers, including *The Life of Jesus* by David Friedrich Strauss, which earned her criticism, as did her very public "living in sin" with the married philosopher and critic George Lewes.

While she gave up her religious beliefs, she did maintain the morals and ethics of Christianity and adopted a philosophy of secular humanism, an important theme in her future works. Her first work of fiction was *Scenes of Clerical Life*, composed of three short stories, after which she began writing the first of seven lengthy novels, *Adam Bede*, which became a huge success.

She took "George" as her pen name, in part as an homage to her paramour, and in part to separate herself from other female writers, because she considered her own work above the romances of her day and wanted to be taken seriously. Of course, she also wanted to get published and have her work reviewed based on its merits, without the fact that she was a woman coming into play. She kept her identity well hidden for her first couple of books, but then several imposters came forward claiming to be the author, even trying to get her royalties. Finally, she had to reveal her identity. By that point the excellent reviews were already in and, as Lewes said, the critics couldn't "unsay their admiration."

Her novels are full of realism, psychological suspense, and colorful characters who are often outsiders, and explore politics in small towns, love, and religion with tremendous affection, wit, and psychological insight. Despite becoming the most successful writer of her era, she was not actively involved in the push for women's rights, and some feel she was unkind to her female characters. Eliot's heroines often led frustrating and restricted lives. Probably because that's how things actually were—perhaps she was just being realistic.

Through her writing, she became the richest self-made woman of her time in England and established a permanent position in the canon as one of the world's greatest novelists.

FURTHER READING

Adam Bede (1859)

The Mill on the Floss (1860)

Silas Marner (1861)

Middlemarch (1871–72)

Daniel Deronda (1876)

My Life in Middlemarch, by Rebecca Meade (2014) (Part memoir, part biography, and part accessible literary criticism, this book shows the relevance of literature to our contemporary lives, using Eliot's masterpiece as its centerpiece.)

THE BRONTË SISTERS

Charlotte (1816–1855), Emily (1818–1848), and Anne (1820–1849)

✦✦✦✦

I am no bird; and no net ensnares me:
I am a free human being with an independent will.

—FROM *JANE EYRE*

Fascination with the three Victorian sisters who lived quietly in the Haworth Parsonage amid the howling winds of the Yorkshire moors, surrounded by a graveyard on three sides, remains undiminished more than two hundred years after their deaths. The Brontë sisters' works, which were distinguished by an emotional intensity that some critics called "coarse," "brutal," and "shocking," remain ranked among some of the best—and most loved—novels ever written. Dark, brooding Rochester and Heathcliff, despite their tyrannical, even abusive behavior, have had an almost hypnotic romantic effect on millions of young women for more than two centuries.

The reclusive lives of these three plain-seeming daughters of a clergyman were a contrast to their vivid imaginations and storytelling. All three sisters died before they were forty in a household—and town—riddled with tuberculosis, where the expected life span was a dire twenty-four years. They lost their mother and two older sisters when they were still young children and lived with their father and brother—also writers and creative souls—in a rigid class system. Despite their literacy, rare for women of their station, the sisters did not have high marriage prospects and were forced to work for a living. They had minimal formal schooling in a severe and spartan school Charlotte used as the model for the Lowood Institution in *Jane Eyre*. And as governesses or teachers to the wealthy's children, they were

miserable—Charlotte called it "wretched bondage"—retreating home and using their degrading experiences and observations as rich material for their work.

As children they were fervent readers; their father insisted on their reading the classics and brought home a box of toy soldiers that they, along with their brother, Branwell, used to create the vivid imaginary worlds of Angria and Gondal, with maps and drawings, rich characters, battles, lady loves dressed in finery, and enough drama that Charlotte would later say that she wrote more before the age of thirteen than as an adult. They put down their stories in little miniature, doll-sized books and also created magazines and staged plays. It is in these stories of fantastical kingdoms, inspired by Charlotte's love of her hero, the Duke of Wellington, and the exotic stories of the Arabian Knights, that the first signs of Edward Rochester appear. The king of Charlotte's make-believe world was the Duke of Zamorna, whom she describes as "passion and fire unquenchable, as impetuous sin and stormy pride, as a young duke—young demon!"

When Charlotte was in school in Belgium, she developed strong feelings for the headmistress's husband, Constantin Héger, writing him totally inappropriate, passionate letters. He rebuffed her, leaving her heartbroken and becoming the basis for characters in *Shirley* and *Villette*.

At twenty, she sent a letter to the poet laureate, Robert Southey, along with some of her poems. He famously wrote back, acknowledging her talent but saying, "Literature cannot be the business of a woman's life, and it ought not to be. The more she is engaged in her proper duties, the less leisure will she have for it." As a result, she paid to have a collection of poetry written by her and her sisters published under their male pseudonyms. Unfortunately, the book sold only two copies. Later she also used the name Currer Bell, when submitting her novel *Jane Eyre: An Autobiography* for publication. It was called "the best novel of the season" despite being "anti-Christian," and its success and the curiosity about its true author allowed her to get her siblings' work published, also under pen names.

Emily, aka Ellis Bell, wrote poetry, most of it religious, despite her belief that "religious fulfillment was to be found in the union of the individual spirit with the eternal spirits in nature." This came to life in the tragic love/ghost story *Wuthering Heights*, which a reviewer described as sickening due to its "details of cruelty, inhumanity, and the most diabolical hate and vengeance" while acknowledging its "powerful testimony to the supreme power of love." Emily rarely left the house or interacted with other people and died of tuberculosis after great suffering at age thirty, just six months after their brother, Branwell, died of it (as well as alcoholism and most likely opium addiction).

Anne, or Acton Bell, was the baby of the family, as well as a poet and author of two novels: *Agnes Grey*, which exposed the exploitation of governesses and the cruelty and materialism of the wealthy, and *The Tenant of Wildfell Hall*, which critiqued married women's lack of legal rights and the double standard for men and women in regard to both education and sexual morality. Two weeks after Emily's death, Anne, too, was diagnosed with tuberculosis and died.

At thirty-eight Charlotte got engaged against her father's wishes (and an initial refusal of her own) to his assistant, Arthur Bell Nicholls, and became pregnant almost immediately. Suffering intense morning sickness, she died from dehydration and malnutrition just months after her marriage.

Charlotte's letters from the time provide some insight into her mindset and character, so much so that after she died her husband begged her friends to burn them because they were "dangerous as Lucifer's matches." Oh, how delicious it would be to read them!

When Charlotte died her profession was listed as "wife" on her birth certificate. She had been married for a few short months and had been writing her entire life.

These sisters, shrouded in mystery, their deaths long attributed to frailty and melancholy—instead of a highly contagious, misunderstood, and stigmatized disease—were actually subversive and revolutionary in establishing passionate, relatable female voices that show undeniable power. They were a lot stronger than history has given them credit for.

FURTHER READING

Charlotte Brontë

Jane Eyre (1846)

Shirley (1849)

Villette (1853)

The Professor (1857)

Charlotte Brontë: A Fiery Heart, by Claire Harman (a biography that covers all three sisters in great depth)

Emily Brontë

Wuthering Heights (1847)

Anne Brontë

Agnes Grey (1847)

The Tenant of Wildfell Hall (1848)

ELIZABETH GASKELL

1810–1865

——◆◆◆◆——

The Brontës may have gone the way of obscurity, like so many other female writers, if it hadn't been for Mrs. Elizabeth Gaskell's *The Life of Charlotte Brontë*, which turned the sisters into icons, securing their literary legacy with what was to become the most famous biography of the nineteenth century. Charlotte, in particular, was a major literary celebrity in her lifetime, and the biography was written to maintain her status at the bequest of her father, Patrick.

> Loyalty and obedience to wisdom and justice are fine; but it is still finer to defy arbitrary power, unjustly and cruelly used— not on behalf of ourselves, but on behalf of others more helpless.

————

Gaskell took on the task but whitewashed the story, leaving out any dark details, such as the possibility that Charlotte used opium (like her brother, who was an addict) in order to achieve her "visions," and her awkward and impassioned advances toward both her headmaster in Brussels and her publisher, George Smith. Instead, Gaskell's biography presented her friend as a model of Victorian female virtue—a respectable and dear daughter, sister, friend, and wife. Gaskell felt it was her duty to maintain Charlotte's reputation so people would continue to read her. *Jane Eyre* did, after all, openly discuss adultery, a madwoman in the attic, the abusive environment of a children's boarding school, and the harsh life of a governess. And the Brontës were such an odd, somber, private little bunch, exposing them to criticism, gossip, and speculation.

The wife of a Unitarian minister and the mother of four children, the respectable Gaskell was inspired to write as a way to deal with the grief of losing her one-

year-old son. The result was her novel *Mary Barton*. Her flair for the melodramatic caught the attention of Charles Dickens, who hired her to write stories for his magazine, *Household Words*.

Her second novel, *North and South*, continued her theme of writing about the "agony of suffering" of the poor, caused by industrialization. She wrote from the perspective of the working class, particularly the factory workers who had flooded Manchester looking for work. The novel's social realism also raised the public's awareness of the dramatic social changes occurring at that time, revealing Gaskell's genuine empathy for the lower classes. While she is mostly forgotten today, known primarily from a television miniseries, *Cranford*, that is based on three of her works, she was a preeminent novelist during her time.

As a mother and a minister's wife, she was able to hide her brave subject matter under the cloak of respectability. Her depictions of prostitution, illegitimacy, fallen women, illness, and tragedy—all stories that challenged commonly accepted views of women and their role in society—demonstrated a progressive humanitarian's heart.

FURTHER READING

Mary Barton (1848)

North and South (1854)

The Life of Charlotte Brontë (1857)

ON THE
USE OF PSEUDONYMS

*I would venture to guess that Anon[ymous], who wrote
so many poems without signing them, was often a woman.*

—VIRGINIA WOOLF

Throughout history women have often used male names or ambiguous initials to publish their works, either to avoid prejudice and criticism or simply because it was necessary in order to get published. Other times they wanted to try writing in a different genre without depending on their already famous real names. There are countless writers who have done this, but here is a list of some of the best-known pen names and the reasons these authors had for using them.

PEN NAME:
GEORGE SAND

REAL NAME:
AMANTINE-LUCILE-AURORE DUPIN DUDEVANT

◆◆◆

When Sand moved to Paris and started mingling with artistic types, she had a short affair with the writer Léonard-Sylvain-Julien Sandeau. The two of them collaborated on articles as well as a novel, her first, *Rose et Blanche*, and they published it under the name Jules Sand. When she was ready to publish her first work of her own, she kept the last name and used George as the first. When *Indiana* came out, launching her successful career, it was under her own nom de plume: George Sand.

PEN NAME:
GEORGE ELIOT

REAL NAME:
MARY ANN EVANS

◆◆◆

Mary Ann Evans had several reasons to write under a male pseudonym. First, she objected to "silly novels by lady novelists" and didn't want to be stereotyped. She also wanted to maintain her privacy, given she was living illegally with a married man. She explained it thus: "By a peculiar thermometric adjustment, when a woman's talent is at zero, journalistic approbation is at the boiling pitch; when it attains mediocrity it is already no more than summer heat; and if she ever reaches excellence, critical enthusiasm drops to the freezing point."

PEN NAME:
"A LADY"

REAL NAME:
JANE AUSTEN

◆◆◆

When *Sense and Sensibility*, Austen's first novel, came out, she published it under "A Lady." She wanted the anonymity, because women who wrote novels suffered from reputational damage and excessive criticism. She hid herself but made it clear to readers that the author was, indeed, female.

PEN NAMES:
CURRER, ELLIS, AND ACTON BELL

REAL NAMES:
CHARLOTTE, EMILY, AND ANNE BRONTË

◆◆◆

The Brontë sisters' publisher told them to use male names or he wouldn't publish their work. Charlotte once said, "We did not like to declare ourselves women, because—without at that time suspecting that our mode of writing and thinking was not what is called 'feminine'—we had a vague impression that authoresses are liable to be looked on with prejudice."

PEN NAMES:
FLORA FAIRFIELD, A. M. BARNARD

REAL NAME:
LOUISA MAY ALCOTT

◆◆◆

Alcott's first poetry and short stories were published in magazines under the name Flora Fairfield. Perhaps she didn't think her work was strong enough just yet. Her lurid gothic thrillers and other "unladylike" works, including *A Long Fatal Love Chase* and *Behind A Mask*, were published under the gender-ambiguous name A. M. Barnard.

PEN NAME:
MARY WESTMACOTT

REAL NAME:
AGATHA CHRISTIE

◆◆◆

After Christie left her cheating husband, she wanted to escape from more than just her marriage; she also wanted to be free from the business of being a famous crime writer. She took her middle name, Mary, and combined it with the last name of some relatives of hers to publish six romance novels, including *Giant's Bread* and *Absent in the Spring*. It wasn't until more than fifteen years later that she was found out by a reviewer. This didn't deter her; she went on to write three more books as Westmacott.

PEN NAME:
HARPER LEE

REAL NAME:
NELLE HARPER LEE

◆◆◆

Okay, this may seem obvious, but dropping her more feminine first name for the more ambiguous "Harper" was done for two reasons. First, Lee thought she would have a better chance of getting published with a name that could have been a man's, and second, she didn't want "Yankees" to take "Nelle Lee" and pronounce it "Nellie." Fair enough.

PEN NAMES:
J. K. ROWLING, ROBERT GALBRAITH

REAL NAME:
JOANNE ROWLING

◆◆◆

When Rowling's first Harry Potter book was accepted by a publisher, they requested that she use initials instead of her first name because they were concerned that a female author might put off their target audience of young boys (never mind that girls were also huge, huge fans of the books). Rowling added her grandmother Kathleen's initial and became J.K. Later, after Potter basically took over the world as a cultural phenomenon, she wanted to write something completely different and distance herself from her famous persona—oh, the pressure! She said she "was yearning to go back to the beginning of a writing career with this new genre, to work without hype or expectation and to receive totally unvarnished feedback." She wrote *The Cuckoo's Calling* under the name Robert Galbraith, and not even her publisher knew she had written it. Her editor thought it really was written by a man! They released the book under the nom de plume to respectable enough sales, but once they revealed the true author, sales went up by 500,000 percent. Now that's the power of a brand in action.

The Mother of Abolitionism
HARRIET BEECHER STOWE
1811–1896

———◆◆◆◆———

The legend goes that when Harriet Beecher Stowe met President Lincoln at the White House in 1862, he said to her, "So you're the little woman who wrote the book that started this great war!" Whether or not that actually happened and despite the mortifying, dated stereotypes in her *Uncle Tom's Cabin*, there is no question that her abolitionist work and writing played an important role in creating awareness of the human cost of slavery.

Originally from Connecticut, Stowe grew up with a strict Calvinist father who came from a family of writers, ministers, and progressive thinkers. Harriet was educated at the Hartford Female Seminary, which taught many of the same courses and subjects as men's schools, and she showed a gift for writing early on. She then married a penniless clergyman; they moved to Cincinnati and had seven children. Despite "the nursery and the kitchen" being her "principle fields of labor," she took up her pen to contribute what she could to the family's income. Her articles appeared in *Godey's Lady's Book*, and she also wrote thirty books over her lifetime, from novels to books on religious faith and homemaking.

Living on the border of Kentucky, Stowe encountered escaped slaves, and after the experiences of attending a slave auction and losing her own son to cholera, she developed deeper empathy for enslaved mothers. She was triggered, in particular, by the forcible separation of families and was inspired to establish her house as a station on the Underground Railroad. When the Fugitive Slave Act of 1850 was passed, it enraged her in its demand that northerners return runaway slaves. Her sister-in-law told her, "Now Hattie, if I could use a pen as you can, I would write something that would make this whole nation feel what an accursed thing slavery is."

Faced with that thrown gauntlet, Stowe began writing *Uncle Tom's Cabin*, publishing it in installments in the abolitionist journal *The National Era* in 1851. Originally popular only in antislavery circles, in 1852 it was released as a book, surprising everyone by selling three thousand copies in its first week, twenty thousand in its first three weeks, and three hundred thousand in its first year in the United States. It became a publishing phenomenon unlike anything the world had seen before. By the time Harriet went to the White House to meet President Lincoln, her book had sold more than two million copies in the United States—and don't just think about that

Women are the real architects of society.

———

in today's terms. Consider that at the time the U.S. population was only 21 million people (compared with 330 million today), and you couldn't just have any ol' book you wanted shipped to you overnight for free.

In the wake of her success, Stowe began touring around the country and world, speaking and donating book proceeds to the antislavery cause. Her "Appeal to Women of the Free States of America on the Present Crisis in Our Country" was a call to arms for the women of the United States to stand up against slavery's cruelty and inhumanity.

Despite the wild popularity and influence of *Uncle Tom*, Stowe received a lot of backlash from white southerners who called her portraits of them inaccurate. An entire industry of southern anti-*Uncle Tom* tomes sprung up. In rebuttal she published *Key to Uncle Tom's Cabin*, which provided all of the historical documents and research that backed up her story. She has also received plenty of criticism for creating the character of Uncle Tom, an enslaved man whom she portrayed as excessively forgiving and obedient. Stowe, who was a devout Christian, created Tom to be a sort of Christ figure, a martyr who sacrificed himself for the greater good of others. She felt that she was being called by God to create awareness of the evils of slavery and demand social change through her storytelling, and Uncle Tom was her conduit. I think it's fair to say mission accomplished.

✦✦✦✦✦✦✦✦✦✦✦✦✦

FURTHER READING

Uncle Tom's Cabin Or, Life Among the Lowly, by Harriet Beecher Stowe, introduction by James M. McPherson (1991)

✦✦✦✦✦✦✦✦✦✦✦✦✦

LOUISA MAY ALCOTT

1832–1888

◆◆◆◆

Generations of girls have seen themselves in the spirited Jo March, who was determined to sail her own ship. *Little Women* immediately struck a chord upon its 1868 publication, after a publisher suggested to Louisa May Alcott that she write "a girl story." It became one of the most enduring and popular books of all time, has been translated into fifty languages, and was adapted into at least six films, several television series, an opera, and a Broadway show. But Louisa May Alcott was so much more than the author of *Little Women* and its sequels.

> There is no easy road to successful authorship; it has to be earned by long and patient labor, many disappointments, uncertainties and trials. Success is often a lucky accident.

Alcott's parents were abolitionists, Transcendentalists, and station masters on the Underground Railroad. Bronson, her zealot father, was an education reformer whose schools consistently sparked controversy, resulting in his being unable to financially support his family. His Temple School in Boston closed after he admitted an African American student and all of the other parents withdrew their own children. He then moved his wife and four daughters to Fruitlands, a society with Utopian goals that included a working farm and commune based on consuming no animal products and using no outside labor. This lasted only seven months—Louisa's mother, Abby, put her foot down after it became clear that she and her daughters would have to keep the "experiment" going by maintaining the house, working the farm, and feeding everyone while the men took long walks in the countryside to discuss philosophy. Sure, this was a Utopia. For the men, at least. Louisa

later wrote a satire of this experience called "Transcendental Wild Oats" that was published in a New York newspaper in 1873.

As a result of her father's inability to provide financial support, the family moved more than twenty times in thirty years. Louisa vowed to pull her "pathetic family" out of poverty and began working at age fifteen, doing any job available: governess, teacher, laundress, seamstress, and eventually, writer. Their most permanent home was Orchard House in Concord, Massachusetts, where they finally settled down from 1858 to 1877, across the street from Ralph Waldo Emerson. It was here that Alcott wrote *Little Women* at a little round "shelf desk" built by her father.

Louisa was educated mainly by Bronson, although Thoreau, Emerson, Nathaniel Hawthorne, and Margaret Fuller—all family friends—also gave her lessons. She had free use of Emerson's extensive library, where she began to read the classics and wrote her first book, *Flower Fables*, in 1854 for Emerson's daughter Ellen. When she submitted an essay called "How I Went Out to Service" about her experience as a governess, it was rejected by publisher James T. Fields, who told her, "Stick to your teaching, Miss Alcott. You can't write." After she proved him wrong, made a bundle, and had publishers fighting over her, she would say that she felt her biggest success was to be able to support her family and let them live in comfort, but she also got a "naughty satisfaction in proving that it was better not to 'stick to teaching' as advised, but to write."

It was important to her to be paid well for her work, so she taught herself how to write stories that would sell. In fact, she was first able to support her family, under the pseudonym A. M. Barnard, writing lurid, gothic thrillers full of love affairs, murder, and opium addiction, such as *Pauline's Passion and Punishment* and *A Long Fatal Love Chase*, which were serialized in magazines.

Her first major literary and commercial success written under her own name was a fictionalized version of her experience working at the Union Hotel Hospital in Georgetown as a military nurse during the first year of the Civil War. Based on her letters home and daily journals, it was a breakthrough piece of writing, opening the public's eyes to the horrors and conditions in the military hospitals. Women had not been allowed to be nurses at first, but this changed as the seriousness and length of the war became clear. Unfortunately, she contracted typhoid pneumonia there and had to return home. Often delusional and poisoned by the mercurous chloride used to treat her, she would suffer from pain, weakness, and hallucinations for the rest of her life. *Hospital Sketches* first appeared in the *Boston Commonwealth*, a weekly newspaper, in four installments in May and June 1863, and later as a book. It was enormously popular, giving a human face to the staggering casualty statistics, and it was also a pioneering account of military nursing.

After her recovery, Alcott accepted the editorship of a children's magazine, *Merry's Museum*, and became its major contributor. When Thomas Niles, a partner at publisher Roberts Brothers, asked her to write a book for girls in 1867, she went into her writer's "vortex" and in mid-July finished Part 1 of *Little Women* for publication that fall. It was an immediate bestseller, and readers clamored for a sequel. Part 2 was published the following spring. Alcott wrote the entire book in less than three months and followed it up with several sequels.

Alcott amassed a fortune with the success of her novels for young adult readers, providing for her parents, siblings, nieces, and nephews and proving that a woman could make a living as a self-trained professional writer. She knew the importance of a profitable book, and she saw that writing children's books was where she could make money, so that's where she continued to invest her time and energy.

Alcott and her mother were also deeply involved in the women's suffrage movement, canvassing door-to-door encouraging women to register to vote. In 1879, Louisa registered as the first woman to vote in the Concord school committee election. Her writing also expressed her views on many of her era's ideas for social reform, including women's rights, racial integration, and education.

Before her premature death at fifty-six, she produced almost three hundred literary works, including stories, novels, plays, poems, sensational thrillers, satires, fairy tales, and gothic novels, but she will always be remembered best for *Little Women*. Jo, the ambitious tomboy who wanted to be a famous writer and live a big life beyond what the world told her she could be, was Alcott's literary doppelgänger. The book still resonates today, with Greta Gerwig's seventh film version released and generations of female artists—from bell hooks to J. K. Rowling to Patti Smith to Simone de Beauvoir—all saying that *Little Women* inspired them and changed what they thought about who they could be. It is timeless in reminding us of our spunky younger selves, full of dreams.

FURTHER READING

The Annotated Little Women, by Louisa May Alcott, edited with an introduction and notes by John Matteson

One Hundred Years Ahead of Her Time

KATE CHOPIN

1850–1904

———◆◆◆◆———

To succeed, the artist must possess the courageous
soul . . . the brave soul. The soul that dares and defies.

———

Unfortunate. *Trite. Sordid. Morbid. Vulgar. Poison.* These are just a few of the words used to describe *The Awakening* when it was first published in 1899 and condemned, dismissed, and banned in Kate Chopin's hometown of St. Louis. At the turn of the twentieth century, sensitive and poetic descriptions of women's inner lives were not considered worthy of literary merit, and writing so frankly about female infidelity and depression was considered outrageous and immoral to readers of the late Victorian era.

The daughter of a French Creole aristocratic mother and a successful and wealthy Irish immigrant merchant father, Kate O'Flaherty received a rigorous education from the nuns at Sacred Heart. She was a beauty, a hilarious mimic, and a lover of music, dancing, and laughter; her successful debut into society resulted in marriage to wealthy cotton merchant Oscar Chopin. The two settled in New Orleans during post–Civil War Reconstruction.

Within eight years, they had five sons and one daughter, then moved to a small French village in northwestern Louisiana, where Oscar operated a general store, after suffering financial hardships. When he died of malaria shortly thereafter, thirty-two-year-old Kate became a widow of little means with six children to raise on her own. After having an affair with a local planter, she moved back to St. Louis, where, after her mother died, she suffered from an overpowering depression. She became involved in literary and cultural circles and started writing to cheer herself up. She wrote more than one hundred short stories and essays, submitting them to magazines, fastidiously tracking their rejections and acceptances and the money she earned from their publication.

Her gifts as a mimic were put to good use in her first two story collections, *Bayou Folk* and *A Night in Acadie*, which reflected her time in Louisiana, using Creole

and Cajun dialect for "local color." Her descriptive writing, use of irony, discussions of subjects such as economic disparity and slavery, and unconventional way of portraying women went unappreciated at the time but have since been recognized as signature features of her work.

The Awakening introduces us to Edna Pontellier, who feels painfully restricted by the limited roles of her gender. Edna P., like so many heroines of the pre-feminism eras, whether Emma Bovary, Anna Karenina, or Lily Barth, is punished for being a woman who desires autonomy and choices beyond that of being wife and mother. Edna has strong existential yearnings, but unfortunately the expectations of society and its conventions create a conflict between what she thinks and feels and how she can behave. The narrator says of her: "At a very early period she had apprehended instinctively the dual life—that outward existence which conforms, the inward life which questions."

On top of acknowledging a rich inner life, Edna makes matters worse by refusing to sacrifice herself for her children *and* by having no-strings-attached sex outside of her marriage. Then, in a fit of loneliness and depression, she dies by suicide.

Of course, the condemnation was swift and harsh, with reviewers writing things like: "to think of Kate Chopin, who once contented herself with mild yarns about genteel Creole life . . . blowing us a hot blast like that." It's a good thing that she didn't send her even racier short story "The Storm" out to publishers. She wrote it the same year and was even more frank in her amoral approach to sexuality (it was finally printed sixty-five years after her death).

It took fifty years after she passed away for critics to begin to notice and try to understand her. In 1969, critic Per Seyersted wrote that in "revolting against tradition and authority; with a daring which we can hardly fathom today . . . she undertook to give the unsparing truth about woman's submerged life."

Although Chopin shocked readers with her subject matter in a society that wasn't quite ready for what she had to say, she is now acknowledged as a writer of astute observation and deep sensitivity and a creator of complex characters whose inner and outer lives are often in conflict.

FURTHER READING

The Awakening and Selected Stories, by Kate Chopin (Penguin Classics edition includes "The Story of an Hour" and "The Storm")

Kate Chopin: A Life of the Author of The Awakening, by Emily Toth

Of the Manor Born
EDITH WHARTON
1862–1937

⬥⬥⬥⬥

E dith Newbold Jones was one of the original "Joneses" the rest of us were meant to "keep up with." Her family's wealth made her part of what a 1929 *New Yorker* article described as "a strict clan making intercellular marriages, attending winter balls, dominating certain smart spots on the eastern seaboard . . . a hard hierarchy of male money, of female modesty and morals." She was restricted, on the one hand, by the prejudices and snobbery of her class and education, but on the other hand she was a subversive thinker, writing critically not only of the greed and materialism she witnessed but also of American foreign policy and capitalism, and perhaps even democracy itself—which is a complicated position to take when you have personally benefited so much from those very things.

Her first major book, the successful *The Decoration of Houses*, was co-written with Ogden Codman Jr. in 1897 in swanky Newport, Rhode Island. *Architectural Digest* called it the King James Bible of interior design and decorating, saying, "Thousands of interior design books have come and gone since, but most, I would argue, merely repackage" Wharton's ideas. She also wrote *Italian Villas and Their Gardens*, illustrated by painter Maxfield Parrish. Her magnificent estate, the Mount, in Lenox, Massachusetts, was carefully designed and curated by her, including a suite of rooms of her own, where she could work with privacy. This is where she wrote *The House of Mirth* and *Ethan Frome*. From that point on, she put out a book a year—forty books in forty years—writing pages every morning and letting them drop to the floor to be organized later, until the end of her life.

She had a couple of failed engagements after her debut at seventeen. Still not married at twenty-three, and almost considered an old maid at that time, she felt she had to marry. Her novels reflect this struggle, criticizing social convention and its consequences: unhappy marriages, secret emotional and sexual longing, and anxiety about making a proper match. Her own marriage to Teddy Wharton was rocky, but because she had her own money—both inherited and earned through her writing—she had a degree of freedom.

She met the journalist Morton Fullerton through her friend the writer Henry James, and fell in love with the bisexual Andover and Harvard man who was breaking hearts across the United States and Europe. She traveled to France with him and, on returning home to her alcoholic, mentally unstable husband, wrote, "I heard the key turn in my prison-lock." She eventually set herself free with a divorce and moved to France, where she stayed for the rest of her life. She returned to the United States only twice, once to receive an honorary doctorate from Yale.

> Life is the only real counselor; wisdom unfiltered through personal experience does not become part of the issue. True originality consists not in a new manner but in a new vision.

During World War I, she stayed in France, dedicating herself to a variety of charitable and humanitarian organizations, and was one of the few journalists and writers reporting from the front lines for American publications. In 1916, she received the French Legion of Honor for her war work.

As a novelist and person, Edith Wharton's style was high energy, steely willed, determined, and elegant. She maintained a writer's imagination and eye from her youngest days, making up lengthy narratives while pacing up and down holding a book before she could even read, to the point that it alarmed her parents, since writing was not considered becoming of a woman of her class. Despite her gifts and accomplishments, her self-doubt and insecurities are well documented, which, given her intense privilege, demanding personality, and the fact that she was the first woman to win the Pulitzer Prize for literature (for *The Age of Innocence*), is somehow refreshing. Maybe there is hope for the rest of us Impostor Syndrome sufferers after all.

Educated by a governess, Wharton spent her childhood traveling through France, Germany, and Italy, where she came to love language, architecture, art, and literature. She also had access to her father's extensive library, saying, "No children of my own age . . . were as close to me as the great voices that spoke to me from books. Whenever I try to recall my childhood it is in my father's library that it comes to life." Known for "always scribbling," she sold her first poem at a church fair at fifteen and privately published her first volume of poems when she was sixteen. At eighteen, she was publishing poetry in the *Atlantic Monthly* and writing novellas.

In 1929 the *New Yorker* published an article that skewered her, mostly for making money writing about her social milieu, claiming she had to leave the country because no one in Boston or New York society would receive her. It seems they were upset at her betraying her social status and, worse, making money from it. *Tres gauche, n'est-ce pas?* But the criticism was directed at Wharton's contempt for much of American culture and self-aggrandizement rather than at her writing, which was clearly exceptional and versatile, as she wrote not only novels, poems, and design books, but also essays, political and travel writing, and literary criticism.

Wharton addressed her critics in a long piece in the *Atlantic* in which she discussed her creative process, claiming that her characters came to her fully formed and even with their own names and that it was exasperating to hear unimaginative responses to her efforts: "It is discouraging to know that the books into the making of which so much of one's soul has entered will be snatched at by readers curious only to discover which of the heroes and heroines of the 'society column' are to be found in it." Although there is no doubt that she wrote in delicious detail about the elaborate social pressures and mores of the Gilded Age in which she grew up, she says her characters created their own tragedies and triumphs, which is why Lily Bart and Undine Spragg and Newland Archer still mesmerize.

◆◆◆◆◆◆◆◆◆◆◆◆

FURTHER READING

The House of Mirth (1905)

Ethan Frome (1911)

The Custom of the Country (1913)

The Age of Innocence (1920)

The Decoration of Houses (1897)

Italian Villas and Their Gardens (1904)

The Writing of Fiction (1925)

Edith Wharton, by Hermione Lee

◆◆◆◆◆◆◆◆◆◆◆◆

Biographer of the Great Divide
WILLA CATHER
1873–1947

What was any art but a mold to imprison for a moment the shining elusive element which is life itself—life hurrying past us and running away, too strong to stop, too sweet to lose.

How does a turn-of-the-century girl from the barren plains of Nebraska with a third-rate education and no connections grow up to become an acclaimed Pulitzer Prize–winning writer? In the case of Willa Cather, it was through self-discipline and study, excellent craftsmanship, strong opinions, an intolerance for mediocrity, fresh subject matter, and the right encouragement at the right time.

The Nebraska of her childhood was a place where you could hear the corn growing, where the stars became godlike guides, where the air of spring could be smelled and felt, and this environment became the cornerstone for much of Cather's writing. But she didn't always feel affection or appreciation for the prairie. She said that it was the happiness and the curse of her life. She was almost forty years old when she finally wrote her first novel. What she became known for writing about was, originally, the thing she couldn't wait to leave behind.

Her family had been farmers in lush Virginia for several generations, but after their barn was suspiciously burned down (during the Civil War half the family fought for the North, the other half for the South, creating animosity in some of their neighbors), they moved to Red Cloud, Nebraska, population one thousand. Willa was nine years old, and her Southern Belle mother left everything behind except the family china, wrapped in Confederate currency. Upon reaching the desolate landscape of the plains, she felt her identity had been erased and once claimed to have cried for a year. She would later write, "There was nothing but land: not a country at all, but the material out of which countries are made."

In the 1880s the population of the western states doubled as hopeful, determined, and fearful immigrants flooded the area in pursuit of a better life. At eleven, Willa took a job delivering mail on horseback, getting to know all of her immigrant neighbors: Swedish, Czech, German, Polish, Russian, Irish, English, and Scottish. Dressed like a boy with a crew cut from the time she was fourteen, she went by the name Willie. She followed the local doctor, whom she idolized, on his house calls, deciding she would go to medical school, unheard-of for a girl. She was home-schooled by her grandmother with an eclectic collection of books they had in the house before going off to the local high school. She had a small room up in the attic, which is where she found solitude and happiness reading Shakespeare and the Romantic poets and studying Latin. By the time she went to the University of Nebraska in Lincoln, she couldn't wait to get out of her small town with all of its stifling limitations.

At college she started out majoring in science, but after a teacher published one of her essays, she became the managing editor of the school paper, *The Hesperian*, writing most of the stories. This would be the start of her journalism career, which would take her to Pittsburgh, where she would teach and write for a women's magazine before moving to New York to become an editor, eventually running *McClure's*, one of the most prestigious magazines of investigative journalism at the time, publishing the likes of Rudyard Kipling, Jack London, and Robert Louis Stevenson. Over six years she became arguably the most powerful woman in journalism and helped turn *McClure's* into one of the most read and most profitable journals of its day. But the grind was starting to get to her.

Her friend and fellow writer Sarah Orne Jewett advised her to turn to fiction, writing to her, "You must find a quiet place . . . You must find your own quiet center of life, and write from that." She was hesitant to take the leap, because her boss, Mr. McClure, had expressed doubt about her future as an author: "He does not think I will ever be able to do much at writing stories, that I am a good executive and I had better let it go at that."

She did eventually dive into the unknown, writing for herself, and the following years saw her create her best written work. Never a conformist, she was living in Greenwich Village, which reminded her of the diverse cultures, colors, and languages of Red Cloud. She was also living with a woman, a fellow editor named Edith Lewis, one of many close but undefined relationships she had with women.

Her debut novel, *O Pioneers!*, was the first of her three Nebraska novels and was published to great critical acclaim. In *O Pioneers!*, *My Ántonia*, and *Song of the Lark*, she drew on her childhood experiences and deep understanding of her neighbors from Red Cloud, writing about the heroic beauty in their struggle as they tried to tame the unforgiving prairie, with its droughts, windstorms, dirt, dust, scorching summers, and subzero winters. In many ways the landscape—at once punishing and exalted—became the heroine of her stories. Through the adventures of her characters, we experience their fear and loneliness on the frontier, homesickness, and longing for connection and come to admire their resilience in their efforts to achieve success—much like Willa's hard work to achieve technical skill as a writer.

In *Song of the Lark* she examines what it takes for a female opera singer to leave a small town to become successful—eventually singing at the Metropolitan Opera in New York, no less—despite disapproval from family and being underestimated by men. She believed, like her character the opera singer Thea Kronberg, that creative women—artists—should not marry, for fear of losing their ability to create. In perhaps her best-known and most beloved work, *My Ántonia*, she assumes the voice of a male narrator, considered audacious at the time, who writes of his admiration for his childhood friend Ántonia, who takes over her struggling family farm after her father's suicide and makes it bear fruit through her own hard work, all while giving birth to and raising her many children.

Cather's work can be viewed as commentary on the dark changes of the first half of the twentieth century: two World Wars, industrialization, the rise of automobiles, manufacturing, and consumerism; the threat of nuclear annihilation; and other developments in science and technology that she found abhorrent. She won the Pulitzer Prize for her World War I novel, *One of Ours*, which also became her first bestseller. She wrote that "personal life becomes paler as the imaginative life becomes richer" even as her photograph graced the cover of *Time* magazine. Her work can also be viewed as commentary on the dark changes of the first half of the twentieth century. Her imagination created a longing for the past of an evolving country, establishing her as a pioneer in American fiction.

＋＋＋＋＋＋＋＋＋＋＋＋＋

FURTHER READING

O Pioneers! (1913)

The Song of the Lark (1915)

My Ántonia (1918)

One of Ours (1922)

The Professor's House (1925)

Death Comes for the Archbishop (1927)

＋＋＋＋＋＋＋＋＋＋＋＋＋

Queen of the Demimonde
COLETTE
(Sidonie-Gabrielle Colette)

1873–1954

——— ✦✦✦✦ ———

Colette is remembered as a libertine, voracious in her life and her work, notorious for her sexual fluidity and almost ridiculously productive. According to her biographer Judith Thurman, she published "nearly eighty volumes of fiction, memoirs, journalism and drama of the highest quality."

In an attempt to understand her complex story, you could say that Colette performed her life in three acts—a shapeshifting drama that began in the French countryside, moved to belle époque Paris (with its demimonde of courtesans and cocottes, actresses, opera singers and dancers, bisexuals, gigolos, artists and intellectuals), and concluded with her in the role of doyenne of *belle lettres*.

In Act One, she is a country girl, growing up in a small village in Burgundy with a great love of nature and an unconventional mother, until she is swept off her feet at twenty by the popular writer Henry Gauthier-Villars, or Willy, a man of the world who taught her its ways. He took his young wife to sophisticated, bohemian Paris and initiated her into his stable of ghostwriters in what Colette later called his "literary factory." The story goes that he locked her in a room and made her write, encouraging her to add racy details to her semiautobiographical coming-of-age stories. These became the famous four *Claudine* novels, which he published under his own name, achieving the status of a bestselling cultural phenomenon. It is clear from the original manuscripts—the ones that were saved by a sympathetic assistant after Willy tried to have them destroyed—that Willy may have been a very good editor but the writing was uniquely Colette's. She left him after thirteen years of marriage and apprenticeship, during which he was repeatedly unfaithful, gave her gonorrhea, and took credit for her work, even selling the *Claudine* copyrights and keeping the profits. Eventually, after a long legal battle, she managed to regain the rights.

In Act Two, Colette appears as scandalously living on the fringes of respectable society when, penniless, she runs off with an aristocratic cross-dresser, Mathilde de Morny, known as Missy, the Marquise de Belbeuf, a descendant of both Louis the IX and Napoleon. Out of necessity, she took to the stage as a music hall dancer, vaudevillian, and performer of pantomime, starring with Missy in *Rêve d'Egypte* at the Moulin Rouge, in which the two shared a passionate kiss. The audience was so outraged they started a riot, and the police shut down the show. All these experiences became material for her new works, including *La Vagabonde*, in which she created a character with no redeeming qualities who was a caricature of Willy.

> Sit down and put down everything that comes into your head and then you're a writer. But an author is one who can judge his own stuff's worth, without pity, and destroy most of it.

———

In Act Three, she is the Grande Dame of French literature, often referred to as the greatest living writer in France. She married the Baron Henry de Jouvenel, editor of the newspaper *Le Matin*, while working as a journalist. Their marriage ended when, after enduring several years of her husband's infidelities, forty-six-year-old Colette seduced her sixteen-year-old stepson. After her second divorce, she pursued several love affairs with both younger men and women, using all of them as inspiration for her fiction.

During World War II, she remained in Occupied Paris, despite the arrest of her (third) husband, writer Maurice Goudeket, who was Jewish. After his release he cared for her in her old age as she suffered from arthritis and was confined to her bed—the "raft" where she continued to write, focusing on themes such as the comforts of nature and a love of animals. The original cat lady, she wrote *La Chatte* and other stories and novellas in which animals are main characters, complete with feelings and the ability to speak.

Some of her most famous books were *Cheri*, published in 1920, about an aging courtesan and her affair with a nineteen-year-old man, and *Gigi*, a 1944 novella that became a successful Broadway play starring Audrey Hepburn (whom Colette handpicked for the role) and the 1958 Academy Award–winning musical film. A celebrity in her own time, Colette was elected the first woman president of the distinguished Goncourt Academy and elected to the Belgian Royal Academy of French Language and Literature, and she was the second woman to become a grand officer of the Legion of Honor.

Behind her provocative dialogue and lush descriptions, she possessed a powerful ability to tap into emotional truth. Her semiautobiographical books about love, marriage, power, and the paradoxes of human intimacy reveal the inner lives of women who are torn between the desire for love and the desire for independence. Although the French literary establishment didn't always approve of her work, and society was often morally outraged at her lifestyle, her psychological insights into women and their behavior have found a broad and enthusiastic audience, from young shop girls to Marcel Proust and everyone in between.

✦✦✦✦✦✦✦✦✦✦✦✦✦✦

FURTHER READING

The Complete Claudine, including *Claudine à l'école* (*Claudine at School*) (1900),

Claudine à Paris (1901), *Claudine en ménage* (*Claudine Married*) (1902), *Claudine s'en va* (*Claudine and Annie*) (1903), and *La Maison de Claudine* (*The House of Claudine*) (1922)

La Vagabonde (1910)

Chéri (1920) and *La Fin de Chéri* (*The Last of Chéri*) (1926)

La Chatte (1933)

Gigi (1944)

Secrets of the Flesh: A Life of Colette, by Judith Thurman

✦✦✦✦✦✦✦✦✦✦✦✦✦✦

Voice of the Old Ways

ZITKÁLA-ŠÁ (RED BIRD)

(Gertrude Bonnin Simmons)

1876–1938

———◆◆◆◆———

Zitkála-Šá was born on the Pine Ridge reservation in South Dakota to her mother, a Nakota Sioux, and a white father who abandoned the family when she was just a baby. Her mother raised and taught her children in the traditional ways of her culture, and Zitkála-Šá spoke Sioux until she was eight, when missionaries came to recruit children for their Quaker Missionary School for Indians in Wabash, Indiana, and gave her the name Gertrude. Her mother thought the offer of education might be the missionaries' way of paying the Native Americans back for taking their land and hoped it would help her daughter survive and advance in the "paleface" world. Also, the missionaries threatened that if she did not send her children to school, her rations would be cut in half.

The experience of forced assimilation was traumatizing to say the least; at school they tied Zitkála-Šá to a chair and cut off her long hair—in her culture short hair was for cowards or people who were mourning—and made her wear clothing that she felt was immodest. They took away her blankets and the beaded dress and moccasins her mother had made for her. She spoke no English.

Feeling isolated from her own culture and suffering cruelty at the hands of the missionaries who blithely tried to assimilate children into their ways, which they deeply believed were superior, she decided to create her own name: Zitkála-Šá, which means "red bird." Her misery eventually turned to anger, and she characterized the students she met later at Earlham College in Richmond, Indiana, as "a cold race whose hearts were frozen with prejudice."

Sioux education was experiential and meant to perpetuate the tribe culture passed on through stories told by the elders. At their mothers' sides, young Sioux girls learned valuable skills from other women, such as how to maintain their arts and crafts, respect elders, care for the sick or unfortunate, be a generous host, respect the dead, and listen to the wisdom of the spirits. Women in Zitkála-Šá's culture, as later depicted in her work, are powerful and inspiring in their maintenance of their traditions.

I will say just what I think. I fear no man—
sometimes I think I do not fear God.

Zitkála-Šá was her school's sole representative at the Indiana State Oratorical contest, presenting a speech regarding the treatment of Native Americans to a bigoted audience who shouted racial slurs at her while she spoke. The oratorical skills she demonstrated at the contest were the start of her work as an advocate for the rights of Native Americans.

She became a schoolteacher and started writing short stories and essays about her life as a Native American, trying to find her identity in a white world. She wrote tales of Dakota legends and folklore that were published in *Harper's* and the *Atlantic Monthly*. The school's founder didn't take kindly to her criticism of boarding school education, calling her "worse than pagan" and describing her writing as "trash," and she was fired.

Her collection of essays *Why I Am Pagan*, written in 1902, explained why Zitkála-Šá rejected Christianity, which she saw as domineering, bigoted, and particularly unfair to women, taking away their power and "enfeebling" them. She wrote, "I prefer to their dogma my excursions into the natural gardens where the voice of the Great Spirit is heard in the twittering of birds, the rippling of mighty waters, and the sweet breathing of flowers. If this is Paganism, then at present, I am pagan."

Feeling as if she didn't fit into either culture, in her writing she tried to marry the two—by taking the oral folklore of Native America and putting it on paper as part of the literate culture in which she had been educated. Some stories were autobiographical; others retold the tales she learned at the feet of her elders, including her favorites about Iktami, or "spider," a trickster whose incidents of bad behavior both were very funny and served as cautionary tales. In 1901, Boston's Ginn and Company published her *Old Indian Legends*, and she became the first Native American woman to bridge the oral traditions of her tribe with the written words of English, without an editor, interpreter, or ethnographer.

Zitkála-Šá was also a talented violinist who studied at the Boston Conservatory of Music and collaborated with composer William F. Hanson on *The Sun Dance Opera*.

For a time, she was the toast of literary circles on the East Coast, but she eventually left to become a clerk at the Standing Rock Reservation, where she married Raymond Talesfase Bonnin, also a Sioux. They lived for fourteen years on the Uintah and Ouray Reservation near Fort Duchesne, Utah, where they had a son and became involved with the Society of American Indians. In 1916 Zitkála-Šá was elected secretary of the organization and they moved to Washington, D.C., where she edited the *American Indian Magazine*. She also founded the National Council of American Indians and played a large role in gaining full citizenship for her people. In her life and in her words, she gave voice to her threatened culture.

◆ ◆ ◆ ◆ ◆ ◆ ◆ ◆ ◆ ◆ ◆ ◆ ◆

FURTHER READING

American Indian Stories, Legends, and Other Writings, by Zitkála-Šá, Introductions by Cathy N. Davidson and Ada Norris (Penguin Classics)

Red Bird, Red Power: The Life and Legacy of Zitkála-Šá, by Tadeusz Lewandowski (American Indian Literature and Critical Studies Series)

◆ ◆ ◆ ◆ ◆ ◆ ◆ ◆ ◆ ◆ ◆ ◆ ◆ ◆

VIRGINIA WOOLF

1882–1941

———◆◆◆◆———

Michael Cunningham, the author of the Pulitzer Prize–winning *The Hours*, a novel based in part on *Mrs. Dalloway*, likened Virginia Woolf to a rock star: "She was doing with language something like what Jimi Hendrix does with a guitar. By which I mean she walked a line between chaos and order, she riffed, and just when it seemed that a sentence was veering off into randomness, she brought it back and united it with the melody."

Woolf's biographer Hermione Lee describes her multiple writing personalities as "difficult modernist preoccupied with questions of form, or comedian of manners, or neurotic highbrow aesthete, or inventive fantasist, or pernicious snob, or Marxist feminist, or historian of women's lives, or victim of abuse, or lesbian heroine, or cultural analyst, depending on who is reading her, and when, and in what context."

Virginia Woolf was a formidable force whose prolific experimental novels, letters, essays, memoirs, and two thousand pages of diaries have earned her mainstay status in women's studies programs and academia. Attempts to explain her and her work have resulted in countless articles, books, and interpretations, which are constantly shifting with the times.

Woolf came of age at the tail end of the Victorian era, a period of tremendous cultural change, and her at-the-time revolutionary literary techniques (stream of consciousness, interior monologue, dream states, nonlinear narrative structures, various points of view) all examined the importance—nay, acknowledged the very existence—of people's inner life. Woolf's point of view focused on thoughts, sensations, memory, and feelings and through it all was unapologetically female.

She was born Adeline Virginia Stephen to one of Britain's most prominent families. Her parents had both been married previously and widowed, and when they married each other they brought together their four children and then went on to have four more, including Virginia. All of the boys received traditional university educations, something not available to her because of her gender, a fact she resented for her entire life and that informed much of her work. She was self-educated and, like so many female writers before her, had access to and read from her father's extensive library. She had the added privilege of being raised in a household full of intellectuals and well-known artists, philosophers, writers, historians, and photographers. She began writing when she was young, creating a humorous newspaper about her family she called *The Hyde Park Gate News*.

There's no doubt in my mind that I have found out how to begin (at forty) to say something in my own voice; and that interests me so that I feel I can go ahead without praise.

———

Woolf sought freedom from traditions, both on the page and in her lifestyle. After her parents' death, she became part of the Bloomsbury Group, a collection of fellow bohemians who congregated to discuss literature and art. It was there that she met Leonard Woolf, also a writer, whom she married despite her fears about the confines of marriage and domestic obligations crushing her creative life. Together they bought a printing press and started Hogarth Press, publishing the works of Katherine Mansfield, T. S. Eliot, Sigmund Freud, and E. M. Forster, as well as their own.

Woolf began to write pioneering works on literary theory and history, focusing specifically on the challenges faced by women writers, their fight to be taken seriously, and the conditions of society that hindered them from becoming part of the English literary canon, in both the past and the present. In *A Room of One's Own*, published in 1929, she famously said that "a woman must have money and a room of her own" in order to be a writer. She describes her two great frustrations: women's lack of access to an education and their financial dependence on men. As her career took off with glowing reviews, celebrity-level attention, and strong sales, she achieved a degree of financial independence that gave her great satisfaction.

Woolf was interested in dualities, and in her novel *Orlando*, the titular protagonist begins the book as a man but later inexplicably wakes up as a woman. She based the character on aristocratic author and diplomatic wife Vita Sackville-West, with whom Virginia had a romantic affair. This "Sapphic" relationship was something that was tolerated, but not understood, by her Bloomsbury Group. In fact, E. M. Forster called lesbianism "disgusting," which Woolf interpreted to mean that he felt women should not be independent from men. Although her affair with Vita eventually ended, they remained close friends.

It was discovered after her death that Woolf was sexually abused by two of her older stepbrothers. She experienced her first mental health crisis at age thirteen, after her mother's death, and would suffer periods of depression and mania that have been diagnosed as what we now understand to be bipolar disorder. One of her twelve psychiatrists believed in a strange theory that mental illness was caused by "focal infection," or infections of the teeth, and subsequently pulled several of Woolf's. She had to wear false teeth after that, which made her both unhappy and suspicious of so-called modern medicine. She once said, "The only way I keep afloat is by working."

During World War II, Virginia and Leonard made a pact that if Germany invaded England, they would die by suicide together, especially given that Leonard was Jewish and they feared the worst. Their London house was destroyed in the Blitz, and the two moved full-time to Monk's House, their home in the countryside. On the verge of "going mad again," thinking she would not recover this time, and not wanting to further burden Leonard, whom she truly loved, she refused medical treatment for her last great battle with depression, filled her coat pockets with rocks, and drowned herself in the River Ouse.

In 1954, upon publication of Woolf's diaries, poet W. H. Auden wrote in an article in the *New Yorker*, "I have never read any book that conveyed more truthfully what a writer's life is like, what are its worries, its rewards, its day-by-day routine." Her legacy, beyond her highly stylized texts, artistic genius, and revolutionary ideas, is that she appreciated and brought to the forefront the female writers who preceded her and became a role model to all who followed her.

FURTHER READING

Mrs. Dalloway (1925)

To the Lighthouse (1927)

Orlando (1928)

A Room of One's Own (1929)

The Waves (1931)

A Writer's Diary, by Virginia Woolf, collected by Leonard Woolf (1953)

The Hours, by Michael Cunningham

BEATRIX POTTER
1866–1943

✦✦✦

Young Beatrix Potter based her characters Peter Rabbit and Benjamin Bunny on her beloved pet rabbits, Benjamin Bouncer and Peter Piper, who she walked on a leash, took with her to Scotland during summer holidays, and first anthropomorphized in a letter she wrote to her former governess's son to cheer him up when he was sick. She drew a little black-and-white sketch and told him, "I will tell you a story about four little rabbits whose names were Flopsy, Mopsy, Cottontail and Peter."

Born in London, Potter always loved to draw and paint, and her schoolroom at home was a menagerie of her pets and other animals she found or captured, including bats, mice, rabbits, lizards, snakes, tortoises, and a hedgehog—all subjects for her art. By the time she was eight, she was filling sketchbooks with her renderings of plants and animals.

Like other well-to-do Victorian young women, she did not have a formal education, but she was taught by her governess and encouraged by her parents to draw. She was invited to study fungi at the Royal Botanical Gardens, where she created hundreds of detailed scientific drawings and wrote a paper, "On the Germination of the Spores of Agaricineae." It was considered good enough to be presented to the all-male Linnean Society, but as a woman Potter couldn't attend, so a member represented her, and it ultimately wasn't published. Potter turned her focus away from botanical illustration to greeting cards and children's books, bringing works such as *Alice in Wonderland* and *Cinderella* to life with her art.

> There is something delicious about writing the first words of a story. You never quite know where they'll take you.

Eventually she created a story around her original rabbit drawing and story from her letter. When the book was rejected by six publishers, she printed 250 copies of *The Tales of Peter Rabbit* for friends and family. It was picked up by publisher and bookseller Frederick Warne, who went through six bestselling printings in the first year and went on to publish the rest of her wildly successful works. *The Tales of Peter Rabbit* and the twenty-eight charming illustrated books that followed

have been translated into thirty-five languages and still sell more than two million (yes, *two million*) copies a year.

Less known is *The Fairy Caravan*, written for older children, which Potter considered "too autobiographical" to be published in England (it was published in the United States first and in the United Kingdom after her death), which is ostensibly about a fantastic animal circus that includes fairies, but is actually a message about protecting and preserving our natural spaces and wildlife.

A smart businesswoman, Potter licensed her creations, creating stuffed animals, tea sets, bedroom slippers, and other products, making Peter Rabbit the oldest licensed literary character. She used her book earnings to buy a working farm in the Lake District, among other properties, and became a conservationist, as well as the first elected female president of the Herdwick Sheep Breeders' Association, eventually leaving four thousand acres of land to the National Trust for Places of Historic Interest or Natural Beauty upon her death.

FRANCES HODGSON BURNETT
1849–1937

◆◆◆

The author of classic favorites *The Secret Garden* and *A Little Princess* began writing as a child. After her father died, her mother was forced to move with her five children to rural Tennessee from Manchester, England, to live with her brother. At sixteen, in an effort to help support her family, Frances started writing stories she modeled on what she had read in women's magazines and had her first one published in *Godey's Lady's Book*. At first, the editor thought that she had plagiarized it because the story was so good, so Frances wrote another to prove her authorship and, over the next few years, started publishing five or six stories per month in periodicals.

After marrying a local medical student and having two sons, Burnett wrote her first novel, *That Lass o' Lowries*, which was serialized by *Scribner's Monthly* and praised in the *New York Herald* with "there is no living writer (man or woman) who has Mrs. Burnett's dramatic power in telling a story . . . it is a red letter day in the world of literature." She was wildly productive and became the family breadwinner (her husband's career never really took off). *Little Lord Fauntleroy*, a children's book about a charming and innocent—and lavishly dressed—little boy, based on her son Vivian, whose velvet and lace suits she had sewn for him when he was small, became a huge bestseller with more than a dozen translations, stage productions, and lots of merch sales.

> With the best that I have in me, I have tried to write more happiness into the world.

———

Interestingly enough, *The Secret Garden* was first published as a book for adults to show how nature, companionship, and a positive attitude were good for children but was not successful (not until after Burnett's death, anyway).

She wrote it based on a real, ivy-covered walled garden she found on the grounds of a mansion she rented in England.

And so, she devoted herself primarily to writing children's literature (perhaps also egged on by the financial success of Louisa May Alcott, whom she met in Boston). A driven and prolific writer, she called herself a "pen-driving machine" and despite her growing popularity she suffered from depression and exhaustion, worn out by her heavy workload and the demands of raising children and running a household.

Flush with royalty payments, she was able to leave the stifling responsibilities of her home life and divorce her husband to travel the world with her sons. She started living an unconventional and lavish lifestyle, becoming something of a sugar mama to an actor ten years her junior, which led critics to claim she had given up "serious" writing for formulaic popular works. The *Washington Post* even wrote that her divorce was a result of her "advanced ideas regarding the duties of a wife and the rights of women." Yes, managing the heavy burden of children and household, supporting an unsuccessful and unhappy husband, and being a writer and breadwinner might make one tired of marriage and domestic responsibilities. Can you blame her? She finally had the money to set herself free. And the public still clamored for more from her.

Burnett published almost thirty novels for children and adults in her lifetime, many of them bestsellers, including a memoir. One of her greatest triumphs was winning a lawsuit after her work was pirated, changing British copyright law and establishing an important precedent for other writers. She lived out the last twenty years of her life on her estate in Long Island with her son Vivian, a graduate of Harvard, working with him as the editor of *Children's Magazine*.

MARGARET WISE BROWN
1910–1952

◆◆◆

The little bunny in his green room winds down and gets ready for sleep by saying goodnight to all that is familiar to him. That comforting ritual of the bunny has been echoed by millions of children and their caregivers who read the book with them each night.

How did Margaret Wise Brown, with no kids of her own, instinctually tap into the needs of young children to create some of the most enduring books of all time and become a pivotal figure in developing children's literature?

A child's own story is a dream, but a good story is a dream that is true for more than one child.

Celeste Ng, author of *Little Fires Everywhere*, told the *Atlantic* how reading Margaret Wise Brown's *Goodnight Moon* became part of her evening routine after her son was born and how she sees its ambiguity as true to her own creative process: "I wonder if one of the reasons that this book remained so popular is that it exists in a kind of sweet spot: It gives you enough guidance to feel secure so that you're not totally adrift. And yet, it also leaves enough space for you to make connections, to start to fill things in for yourself. It doesn't try to give you a specific story."

Born to wealthy parents and raised in Brooklyn and suburban Long Island, she attended Hollins College in Virginia and became a teacher at the progressive Bank Street College of Education, helping to shape the curriculum. She seemed to know what small children wanted as both a writer and children's book editor, guided in part by her association with Lucy Sprague Mitchell, who founded the Bank Street model of education that nurtured the "whole child."

It was while teaching that Brown wrote her first story for little ones, *When the Wind Blew*. She and Mitchell eventually enlisted several writers to put together a collection of children's stories called *Another Here and Now Story Book*. This led to Brown launching her own publishing company called William R. Scott, where she became a pivotal figure in the Golden Age of children's publishing, a progressive movement that created books that appealed specifically to children's sensibilities and imagination. She wrote more than one hundred books and, as an editor, commissioned countless others, including Gertrude Stein's children's book *The World Is Round*. She used her success and influence to help children's book writers and illustrators establish and fight for their rights and fair contracts with publishers.

Unlike many of her picture book peers, Brown was a writer first, not an illustrator, and she was the first person to write books specifically for children five and under. She wrote in a musical, rhyming manner and told people that her books came to her in dreams.

A rebel and adventurer, movie-star gorgeous, and absurdly prolific, she had complicated relationships with both men and women, including actor John Barrymore's ex-wife, the actress Blanche Oelrichs. At the time of Brown's premature death at age forty-two of an embolism, she was engaged to James Stillman Rockefeller Jr. of, yes, *those* Rockefellers (and Carnegies too).

Her biographer Amy Gary says that when Brown died there was a treasure trove of "manuscripts and ideas for books that were years ahead of their time" and that, in addition to many other things she learned by studying Brown's life, ultimately she learned "how to live with awe and to love with abandon." Just like a child.

LUCY MAUD MONTGOMERY
1874–1942

◆◆◆

There are many parallels between Maud (without an "e," as she preferred) Montgomery and Anne, her spunky, book-loving heroine with the red braids. They both found solace in the outdoors and exploring the natural treasures of Prince Edward Island. They both were orphans (at least effectively—Maud's father moved across the country and remarried after her mother died of tuberculosis, when she was not even two, leaving her with her maternal grandparents), and both lived with elderly caregivers somewhat isolated from society and with many imaginary friends.

Before the huge success of *Anne of Green Gables*, Montgomery was educated in a one-room schoolhouse. She wrote that it was near a grove that was "a fairy realm of beauty and romance to my childish imagination . . . it was a stronger and better educative influence in my life than the lessons I learned at the desk in the schoolhouse." She started writing poetry at a young age, including a poem at age nine about her favorite birch tree. At sixteen she published "On Cape LeForce" in *The Patriot* on a visit west to stay with her father, which delighted her on what was otherwise an unpleasant visit to the parent who abandoned her. She returned home and received her teacher's license from Prince Wales College, graduating with honors and completing a two-year program in just one year. She lived as her grandmother's caregiver for thirteen years while teaching and working as a proofreader at the *Daily Echo* in Halifax and at the local post office, where she mailed her submissions of stories and poems to magazines and publishers in secret under pen names, including Joyce Cavendish and the ambiguously gendered L. M. Montgomery.

Anne of Green Gables was rejected by six publishers, and Montgomery became so frustrated she threw the manuscript in a hat box, where it sat for two years before she sent it out again. This time she obtained a contract with the Page Company of Boston, and the book became a bestseller, selling nineteen thousand copies in its first five months. Of course, then, they wanted sequels—why kill the golden goose?—and, despite the fact that Montgomery didn't want to "write [Anne] through college," she was contractually bound to continue, which resulted in six books in total before she was free to write about something else.

> I am simply a "book drunkard." Books have the same irresistible temptation for me that liquor has for its devotee. I cannot withstand them.

———

She married a Presbyterian minister and they had three sons, one of whom was stillborn. She managed, through her grief and while constantly writing, to raise children, run a household, help with her husband's ministry, and battle depression—both her husband's and her own.

Montgomery's work all took place on P.E.I., with the exception of *The Blue Castle*, a bestselling adult novel that was banned by some libraries because the main character is a rebellious unwed mother who switches religions.

One of the most popular Canadian writers and one who is loved by Mindy Kaling, Margaret Atwood, Alice Munro, and millions of others, Montgomery wrote twenty books, which have been translated into thirty languages with countless film, television, and stage adaptations. She was the first Canadian woman to become a member of the Royal Society of Arts and Letters. Her last Anne book, *The Blythes Are Quoted*, was delivered to her publisher the day before she died and languished in a vault until 2009, perhaps because of its (unpopular) pacifist message at the peak of World War II. She also left behind thousands of pages of journals, photography, memoirs, and a collection of short stories that spans diverse genres revealing the amazing breadth of her talents.

LAURA INGALLS WILDER
1867–1957

◆◆◆

For Laura Ingalls Wilder, growing up as a real-life pioneer girl—facing near starvation, blizzards, the longest winter ever (an actual historical event studied by fascinated scientists who couldn't believe its harshness), drought, the death of her baby brother, illness, and a plague of locusts of biblical proportions (3.5 trillion, to be exact; one of the most devastating natural disasters in U.S. history, causing billions of dollars in damage)—was even more difficult than her life as she fictionalized it in her classic, wildly popular, and culture-shaping *Little House* books.

As in the books and popular TV series, Laura's parents were Charles and Caroline Ingalls. She spent the first years of her life on a farm in Wisconsin, then in Missouri, Kansas, Minnesota, and Iowa. Her older sister, Mary, did go blind after an illness, and her baby brother, Freddie, died at nine months old. The family eventually moved to Walnut Grove, Minnesota, where the books take place.

For more than sixteen years, the would-be homesteaders traveled by covered wagon and sojourned in railroad towns through the Great Plains during the post–Civil War western expansion. Wilder became a teacher and started her writing career with columns in farming journals to help supplement her income.

She didn't begin to write her life story down until after losing everything in the stock market crash of 1929. By that time, Wilder was in her early sixties and was urged on by her daughter, Rose Lane Wilder, a journalist, who served as her editor and had contacts in the publishing world. Wilder's memoir, *Pioneer Girl*, portrayed events as they actually were. Charles Ingalls never made it as a farmer, and there were times when the family lived as squatters on the Osage Indian reservation or homeless in Iowa, drifting from rented room to room in a sketchy town. There was a time when she was living with and caring for a sick woman whose alcoholic husband came home drunk one night and almost molested young Laura. Wilder and her husband, Almanzo, both suffered from diphtheria; he had a stroke, leaving him disabled, their second child died a month after his birth, and they dealt with

As you read my stories of long ago I hope you will remember that things truly worthwhile and that will give you happiness are the same now as they were then. It is not the things you have that make you happy. It is love and kindness and helping each other and just plain being good.

———————

drought, fire, and financial hardship.

The manuscript was rejected by publishers until a children's book editor asked her to rewrite it for a "juvenile" audience. Wilder and her daughter made the revisions, and that first book, *Little House in the Big Woods*, started a phenomenon. Wilder would ultimately write nine books in the series, and the wildly popular *Little House on the Prairie* television series that aired from 1974 to 1983 created such a passionate base of fangirls that there is now an annual Laurapalooza in Wisconsin, where she was born.

So, while based on her life and true in spirit, her books are not necessarily meant to be factual autobiography. What Wilder did acknowledge was that her adventures as a child took place during an important part of American history, and her works bring that time period to life, in all its Manifest Destiny optimism, for better or worse.

AGATHA CHRISTIE

1890–1976

⬩◆◆◆◆⬩

Her favorite murder weapon was undetectable, tasteless poison: arsenic, belladonna, cyanide, hemlock, strychnine, or thallium, many of which killed the victim with symptoms similar to those of food poisoning or cholera or through asphyxiation. Iconic mystery writer Agatha Christie wasn't a fan of bloody violence. Rather than a knife or gun, her weapon of choice was more likely to be a cup of tea, cough syrup, marmalade spread on a scone, or birthday cake icing—poisons were used in more than thirty of her sixty-six murder mysteries. She was well schooled in them and wrote with great scientific precision. During World War I, before becoming a writer, she studied as an apothecary, learning to make compounds by hand working in a dispensary and hospital.

It's hard to believe that her writing career began after a bet with her sister, Madge, herself a writer, who didn't think Agatha could pen a good detective novel. After much labor, and after six publishers rejected it, *The Mysterious Affair at Styles* became Agatha's first published work; she was twenty-six. *The Pharmaceutical Journal*, of all places, wrote an unexpected review, praising her for her accuracy.

Her clever, pacifist detectives—the brilliant, well-fed, heavily mustachioed Hercule Poirot and the deceptively unassuming gray-haired spinster Miss Marple—are beloved, so much so that Poirot received his own obituary in the *New York Times* when Christie killed him off in 1975—one year before her own death—after he had appeared in thirty-seven of her books.

Agatha Mary Clarissa Miller was born in southwestern England. Her father was an American stockbroker who homeschooled her, and she didn't receive any formal education until she was sent to finishing school in Paris at sixteen. As the youngest child, she taught herself to read at the age of five and spent her childhood living among imaginary friends, reading Louisa May Alcott, Edith Nesbit, and countless American thrillers, and began writing poetry and telling stories to keep herself amused. At eleven she published her first poem in a local newspaper; she had written it while in bed with the flu, where her mother told her to write her stories down.

She often found inspiration for plots and characters in people she saw on her day-to-day walkabouts, at the train station, or in a shop. She would jot down her notes, ideas, and character concepts and work out plots and clues in endless notebooks before she sat down to write.

Imagination is a good servant and a bad master.
The simplest explanation is always the most likely.

———

She fell madly in love and married aviator Archie Christie, and the two took an extended honeymoon on an official tour of the British Empire, visiting South Africa, Australia, New Zealand, and Canada with a stopover in Oahu. She learned to surf, becoming one of the first Brits to do so. She had the couple's only child, Rosalind, and had her first book published, part of a five-book contract, all in short time. But there was a war going on, and with her working at the hospital and her husband away as a fighter pilot, they didn't get much time together.

One of the great mysteries of Christie's own life, and one she never spoke of after it happened, was her own disappearance for ten days after Archie told her he was in love with another woman and wanted a divorce. By then she was a famous writer, and so her humiliation ended up on the front pages of the tabloids and even the *New York Times*. One evening, she kissed her daughter good night, got in her car, and vanished, launching one of the biggest manhunts in history, with a thousand policemen on the search, including Sir Arthur Conan Doyle, who summoned a medium to use paranormal powers to locate her. Her abandoned car was located, and there was speculation that she had drowned or been murdered by her husband, among other wild theories. She was eventually located, safe and sound, checked into a spa hotel under the name of her husband's mistress. After she was discovered and the press calmed down, blaming the incident on amnesia, shock, or a suicidal "fugue," she ended up divorcing Archie, moving with her daughter to the Canary Islands, and writing more and more books.

It was during this time that she started to write something completely different: romance novels, six in all—partially for money and partially to escape being "Agatha Christie"—under the pseudonym Mary Westmacott.

She had always wanted to travel on the famed luxury train the Orient Express, and so she set off solo, to Baghdad, where she met her next husband, the fourteen-years-younger archaeologist Max Mallowan. They traveled together on many archaeological digs, to Syria and Iraq, and she learned photography, cleaning his artifacts with her face cream and memorializing them with pictures. Their travels, especially her multiple train trips, inspired one of her most famous novels, *Murder on the Orient Express*, published in 1934.

Her play *The Mousetrap* was originally a radio script written as an eightieth birthday gift for Queen Mary; it opened on the London stage in 1952. Although it isn't Christie's best work, it holds the record for the longest-running play in the world. It is still playing today—almost seventy years later. Part of its popularity may stem from the fact that it directly engages viewers in the effort not to reveal the twist ending. At the end of each performance, an actor addresses the audience, saying, "Now you have seen *The Mousetrap* you are our partners in crime, and we ask you to preserve the tradition by keeping the secret of whodunit locked in your hearts." Christie's last public appearance was at the *Mousetrap* annual party in 1974, when she was eighty-four.

She became a dame—the female version of being knighted—in 1971 and passed away, peacefully and quietly, in 1976.

Her work endures, as readers revel in the pleasure of solving her brilliant puzzles, where ordinary people are driven by desperate circumstances, not psychopathy, to rationally, meticulously plot murder. She is the best-selling novelist of all time, with two billion copies of her books in print.

◆◆◆◆◆◆◆◆◆◆◆◆◆◆◆

FURTHER READING

The Mysterious Affair at Styles (1920)

The Murder of Roger Ackroyd (1926)

Murder at the Vicarage (1930)

Murder on the Orient Express (1934)

The A.B.C. Murders (1936)

Death on the Nile (1937)

And Then There Were None (1939)

Evil Under the Sun (1941)

Five Little Pigs (1942)

Crooked House (1949)

◆◆◆◆◆◆◆◆◆◆◆◆◆◆◆

ZORA NEALE HURSTON

1891–1960

———— ♦♦♦♦ ————

It was Alice Walker who revived her from the dead. "Looking for Zora," her introduction to *A Zora Neale Hurston Reader*, tells how, in 1973, she walked through waist-high, snake-infested weeds at a segregated cemetery, the Garden of Heavenly Rest in Fort Pierce, Florida, to place a simple gray headstone inscribed "Zora Neale Hurston: Genius of the South. Novelist, folklorist, anthropologist" on the unmarked grave.

Hurston, despite being the most significant black female writer in the first half of the twentieth century, never made any real money while she was alive, and she often received both racist and sexist reviews. Now that's intersectionality at work. *Native Son* author Richard Wright said of her masterpiece, *Their Eyes Were Watching God*, "The sensory sweep of her novel carries no theme, no message, no thought." According to biographer Valerie Boyd, the largest royalty check Hurston earned for a book was just $943.75. And, in 1950, ten years before her death, a *Miami Herald* reporter saw her working in the suburbs as a maid for thirty dollars a week. When she died from a stroke in a welfare home in 1960, her neighbors took up a collection to pay for the funeral but didn't have enough for a headstone, hence the unmarked grave. Regarding the treatment of black female writers in the early to mid-twentieth century, Walker once wrote that it was "cruel enough to stop the blood."

Hurston grew up in Eatonville, Florida, the first township incorporated by and for black people. She sometimes clashed with her preacher father, who felt she was too spirited, but her mother always encouraged her and her siblings to "jump at da sun." She would revisit her hometown again and again in her fiction. Zora's mother died when she was thirteen, and things took a bad turn—she almost killed her father's new wife in a fistfight and left home.

At twenty-six, with no high school education, she passed herself off as ten years younger, and she never added the years back on. She eventually made her way to

New York, arriving in Harlem with $1.50 and one published short story to her name. She enrolled, the only black woman, at Barnard College, and graduated in 1928 at age thirty-six (although she claimed to be twenty-six). She went on to do graduate work in anthropology at Columbia University.

The scrappiness and resourcefulness that got her from Eatonville to Columbia also helped her become a major figure in the Harlem Renaissance. In addition to her unique, lyrical voice and powerful storytelling, she had great charm and intelligence, a sense of humor, and a larger-than-life personality. She also looked fabulous in a hat and cut quite a stylish figure. Her many talents helped her find funding for her work. She became friends with poet Langston Hughes, and the two of them shared a patron, Charlotte Osgood Mason, a white Manhattan socialite and philanthropist, who gave them each a monthly stipend (Zora called Mason a "Negrotarian").

> I belong to no race or time. I am the eternal
> feminine with its string of beads.

In 1927 Hurston and Hughes traveled through the South in her coupe, "Sassy Susie," on an adventure Hughes described as "a collector's trip for one of the folk-lore societies. Blind guitar players, conjur men, and former slaves were her quarry, small town jooks and plantation churches, her haunts. I knew it would be fun traveling with her. It was." He didn't mention that she also kept a pearl-handled revolver in a shoulder holster, aware of the dangers of traveling by car through the South while black.

Back in New York, the thrice-divorced Hurston fell into "the real love affair of my life" with a brilliant man twenty years younger. During their tumultuous relationship, he tried to convince her to marry him and give up her career. He wanted a wife who would look after him. Despite her great love for him, she was flummoxed by this request, saying, "I had things clawing inside of me that must be said, I could not see that my work should make any difference in marriage."

Hurston received a Guggenheim Fellowship to travel to Jamaica and Haiti, where she immersed herself in studying the native practice of Vodou. She also did six months of fieldwork in New Orleans as an initiate, not just an observer, bringing the reader right into the experience of the esoteric religion, its rituals, ceremonies, and spells, which she wrote about in "Hoodoo in America," which appeared in 1931 in *The Journal of American Folklore*, and her nonfiction books *Mules and Men* and *Tell My Horse*.

It was during her time in Haiti that Hurston wrote the work she would become best known for, *Their Eyes Were Watching God*, about an unapologetic, independent woman in love who refuses to be victimized. In a passionate frenzy, she completed the manuscript in just seven weeks.

The reaction to its publication in 1937 was mixed. The traditional press, such as the *New York Times*, praised it and gave it a lot of positive attention, but the (male) black literary community trashed it. They dismissed it as lightweight, complaining that she should focus more on social issues and white racism in her work. But her stories that resonate the most are those of everyday, rural black women who overcome the many obstacles put in front of them and come into their own. She also wrote in colloquial Southern dialect, which her peers claimed reinforced black stereotypes. Richard Wright, her longtime literary rival, whose work was "protest fiction," even called it a "minstrel show." These criticisms may explain why her work disappeared from the literary canon for two decades after her death.

And yet she had tremendous pride in black culture and heritage and wrote almost exclusively about the black experience. In her 1950 article "What White Publishers Won't Print" she wrote, "I have been amazed by the Anglo-Saxon's lack of curiosity about the internal lives and emotions of the Negroes . . . above the class of unskilled labor."

Since her rediscovery in the 1970s by Alice Walker, all of Hurston's books are back in print and available around the world. In 2018 Hurston's last book, *Barracoon*, was published for the first time. The book is based on her 1927 interviews with the last surviving African brought to the United States as a slave. It topped many best books of the year lists and was a *New York Times* bestseller.

◆ ◆ ◆ ◆ ◆ ◆ ◆ ◆ ◆ ◆ ◆ ◆ ◆ ◆

FURTHER READING

Jonah's Gourd Vine (1934)

Their Eyes Were Watching God (1937)

Dust Tracks on a Road (1942)

Barracoon: The Story of the Last "Black Cargo" (2018)

I Love Myself When I Am Laughing . . . and Then Again When I Am Looking Mean and Impressive, edited by Alice Walker and Mary Helen Washington (1979)

◆ ◆ ◆ ◆ ◆ ◆ ◆ ◆ ◆ ◆ ◆ ◆ ◆ ◆

MARGARET MITCHELL

1900–1949

◆◆◆◆

What quality is it that makes some people able to survive catastrophes and others, apparently just as brave and able and strong, go under?

W hen Margaret Mitchell won the Pulitzer Prize for *Gone With the Wind* in 1937, she beat out William Faulkner's *Absalom, Absalom!*, and, despite its being considered a classic, critics have been arguing about the book's literary merit ever since. As Scarlett O'Hara would say, brushing off such nonsense, "Fiddle dee dee." The story has a complicated legacy; it romanticizes the antebellum South, portraying racist stereotypes of black people and minimizing the horrors of slavery, but it also created one of literature's most memorable heroines, the indomitable survivor Scarlett O'Hara. It also detailed the horrors of the Civil War and Reconstruction in more than one thousand pages of deeply researched detail, all in the guise of a romance.

Margaret Munnerlyn Mitchell was a fourth-generation Atlantan of Irish heritage whose grandfather fought in the Civil War. Her mother encouraged her to read the classics and write her own stories, and from the time she could talk and hold a pencil she was writing tales and plays and performing them for friends and family. By age eleven she had already read all of Shakespeare's works.

Her mother was a founding member of the League of Women Voters in Georgia and took Margaret to suffragette rallies. After graduating from the prestigious finishing school Washington Seminary, she spent one year at Smith College, but when her mother died, she returned home to take care of her father and the household. She made a traditional debut into society and became known as a flirt and was turned down by the Junior League when she performed the scandalous Apache dance popular in Paris nightclubs at a ball.

Her first husband, Berrien "Red" Kinnard Upshaw, is widely believed to be the model for the handsome and dangerous Rhett Butler. But Red was a little *too* dangerous, as well as violent, and the marriage ended after only a couple of months.

As a journalist at the *Atlanta Journal Sunday Magazine*, Mitchell wrote 129 feature stories in four years. After breaking her ankle and being forced to stay home, she started what would become *GWTW*; it would take her ten years to finish. She told an interviewer that she knew her details so well not only because she grew up hearing the stories from people who had lived through the war, but also because she "read the files of old newspapers from 1860 to 1878 and I read hundreds of old magazines, diaries and letters. And I don't know how many hundreds of books I consulted. Those books were on every subject from mid-Victorian architecture to how far a Confederate rifle would shoot."

In 1930 an editor from Macmillan was visiting Atlanta and Mitchell showed him around town. He asked about her manuscript and she demurred, until his last night in Atlanta, when a friend snidely remarked that Margaret wasn't serious enough to write a successful novel, which made her angry enough to share it. He read it on the train home and knew it was "something of tremendous importance." She received a $500 advance.

To say that *GWTW* became a phenomenon is an understatement. Before it was even published in 1936, big-shot Hollywood producer David O. Selznick bought the film rights for the highest amount ever paid for a book: $50,000. The movie's premiere in Atlanta was a major event, and the film won the Academy Award for best picture in 1939.

The popularity of *GWTW* made Mitchell a celebrity, and she was in high demand. She also received endless fan mail and answered every letter personally. When World War II broke out, she volunteered for the Red Cross and financed the outfitting of a hospital ship. She also anonymously set up scholarships for black medical students at Morehouse College.

She never did publish another book. We know she wrote a ghost story set on an old pre–Civil War plantation and a gothic novel, but she had all of her manuscripts destroyed. In 1949 she was struck by a speeding taxi on Peachtree Street and died five days later; the entire city of Atlanta mourned.

GWTW has now sold more than twenty million copies and been translated into twenty-nine languages. Scarlett, whether an ideal role model or not, is a fierce and gutsy heroine for the ages (and, yes, I did have a six-foot-tall life-size black-and-white poster of Clark Gable as Rhett on my bedroom door as a girl several decades after the movie and book were released. P.S.: I wasn't the only one.)

FURTHER READING:

Gone With the Wind, by Margaret Mitchell (1937)

RACHEL CARSON

1907–1964

——— ✦✦✦✦ ———

The aim of science is to discover and illuminate truth.
And that, I take it, is the aim of literature, whether
biography or history or fiction; it seems to me, then,
that there can be no separate literature of science.

———

Sixty years before Al Gore's *An Inconvenient Truth* documentary and book hit movie screens and the bestseller lists, writer, marine biologist, and ecologist Rachel Carson was addressing the dangerous half-truths of the chemical industry and negligent government policy in her groundbreaking book *Silent Spring*. Her writings about the dangers of pesticides, particularly DDT, became the catalyst that led to the creation of the U.S. Environmental Protection Agency and a ban on dangerous man-made chemicals. Her previous works focused on the beauty of the ocean and the interconnectedness of all creatures in nature and were written with a lyrical sense of wonder. Her witness to nature's destruction compelled her to reluctantly speak out, creating a major shift in the public's awareness of how human hubris and "progress" were destroying the world.

Carson grew up on a sixty-five-acre farm in rural Pennsylvania, spending her younger days exploring nature and writing. She read Beatrix Potter and became particularly fascinated by birds, writing about wrens, bobwhites, orioles, hummingbirds, and cuckoos.

Always a writer, she said, "I can remember no time, even in earliest childhood, when I didn't assume I was going to be a writer." She went to the Pennsylvania College for Women, majoring in English, but by the time she graduated in 1929 she had changed her focus to biology. She received her master's from Johns Hopkins University, specializing in the American eel. Her mother sold apples, chickens, and the family china to help pay for Carson's education. When her ailing father died,

followed shortly thereafter by her divorced sister, she became the sole financial support for her mother and her two young nieces. Carson worked as a lab assistant and taught biology and zoology, and was eventually forced to leave graduate school to get a better-paying job at the Bureau of Fisheries, while selling articles to the *Baltimore Sun* for extra income.

It was during her time working at the U.S. Fish and Wildlife Service that she found her beloved subject matter: the ocean and its many wonders. Part of her job was to create educational seven-minute radio scripts about marine life called "Romance Under the Waters" and pamphlets on conservation; she eventually became editor in chief of all publications for the agency. One of her first brochures was deemed too poetic:

> *To stand at the edge of the sea, to sense the ebb and the flow of the tides, to feel the breath of a mist moving over a great salt marsh, to watch the flight of shore birds that have swept up and down the surf lines of the continents for untold thousands of years, to see the running of the old eels and the young shad to the sea, is to have knowledge of things that are as nearly eternal as any earthly life can be.*

Her supervisor encouraged her to submit the brochure's essay to the *Atlantic Monthly*, which published it as "Undersea" in 1937. It was expanded into her first book, *Under the Sea Wind*.

Still working her day job and supporting her family, including adopting and raising her grandnephew and all that required, she wrote at night, agonizing over a new book so broad and detailed in its research that she began calling it "Out of My Depth" and "Carson at Sea." *The Sea Around Us*, first serialized in the *New Yorker*, became an instant sensation, landing on the *New York Times* bestseller list for eighty-six weeks. It was translated into thirty-two languages and won the National Book Award in 1952.

This all made her both rich and famous, and she was able to leave her job to write full-time as well as to buy a piece of land in Maine overlooking the sea, where she built a cottage.

Amazingly, despite writing three additional books about the beauty of the ocean, she never learned to swim, didn't like boats, and as a child never even saw or smelled the ocean. She preferred the tidal pools near the shore.

Her work culminated in *Silent Spring*, which the *New Yorker* serialized in 1962. It took her four painstaking years to write, as she sifted through the research and wrote in almost mythological terms about the devastation that pesticides wrought. She clearly explains the way chemicals are transferred from animal to animal, growing in concentration and showing up even in human breast milk. She opens the book with a parable about a hypothetical town that suffers the consequences of pesticides and asks what life would be like if there were no birds singing, if there were nothing but silence. *Silent Spring* also raised larger questions about whether or not humans have the right to control nature. Throughout the difficult writing of this, her seminal work, Carson was dying from breast cancer.

The chemical industry began a propaganda campaign to discredit her, her publisher was threatened with legal action, and she was called a "hysterical woman," a "spinster," an "alarmist," and a "communist." It was a battle of sorts between the masculine chemical scientists who worked in the lab and the "softer" female scientist doing her work in nature. Sponsors of her CBS special, `The Silent Spring of Rachel Carson`, pulled out at the last minute, but the network went ahead and aired it anyway, reaching fifteen million viewers. Her calm, rational demeanor raised the public's consciousness and started a movement. In 1963, President John F. Kennedy called for a congressional hearing regarding the regulation of pesticides. Despite suffering side effects and exhaustion from radiation treatments, Carson testified to a rapt audience, wearing a heavy brown wig to hide her baldness.

Carson died eighteen months after *Silent Spring* was published. Her brave and loving work not only elevated nature writing and had tremendous impact and moral vision, but also showed us our place in the larger world and the fluidity and transience of life. She turned plankton into poetry and started a conversation about our role, and moral responsibility, as humans, knowing that man's efforts to control nature were also a war against himself, and one that he would lose. Carson comingled science with literature and a strong conscience and showed that science and art don't have to be mutually exclusive.

+ + + + + + + + + + + + +

FURTHER READING

`Under the Sea Wind` (1941)

`The Sea Around Us` (1951)

`The Edge of the Sea` (1955)

`Silent Spring` (1962)

+ + + + + + + + + + + + +

The Greatest Living Writer in the South
EUDORA WELTY
1909–2001

At the time of writing, I don't write for my friends or myself, either; I write for "it," for the pleasure of it.

Reading Eudora Welty feels like sitting on a chair on the front porch in the heat, swatting away the flies while listening to someone tell a wicked and sly story that would have you laughing out loud one minute and feeling a terrible sadness the next. You can almost hear the whirring of the overhead fan and the clinking of the ice cubes against your glass of sweet tea. Her words, like her photographs, are atmospheric, evoking a specific time and place, as well as a feeling. The feeling of home. But a home full of quirks, misunderstandings, and specific ways of speaking and behaving.

One of her most famous stories is called "Why I Live at the P.O.," referring to the post office, but she could have written one called "Why I Live at the Library." As a child in Jackson, Mississippi, she went to the library every day and read so much the stern librarian limited her to two books a day. That same library would eventually be renamed in her honor. Her mother, a former schoolteacher, loved language and books so much she was known for refusing to leave her burning house until she saved her Charles Dickens novels.

Welty led a quiet life, living in the same house she grew up in for more than seventy years. Her neighbors could hear her click-clacking away on the typewriter upstairs through her open window. She didn't believe in air-conditioning and liked the fresh air to experience the seasons. She also tended to the roses and camellias in her garden, kept up on current events, and would welcome unannounced visitors who were looking for her to sign their books, giving them a glass of bourbon and a home-cooked meal.

She was no tortured artist seeking out glamour, publicity, or notoriety, although, for the last forty years of her life, after William Faulkner died, she was often called "the greatest living writer in the South." Her genius expressed itself in the most

intimate and perhaps most complex thing in life—the family unit—with all its individual peculiarities.

After college, graduate school at Columbia University, travel through Europe, and a stint in San Francisco, she returned to Jackson when her father died in 1930 and never left again. She worked at a radio station, as a society columnist, and as a publicity agent before taking a job she said was invaluable to her writing, as a photographer for the Works Progress Administration. Traveling through the backroads of Mississippi, she immortalized the lives of people during the Depression. Like her photography, her writing didn't overly explain—it simply revealed. Her travels on the Natchez Trail and Mississippi River would become the subjects of much of the work that came after.

She edited her writing much like a seamstress or quiltmaker, cutting parts of the manuscript out, then moving them and pinning the pieces where she felt they worked better.

In 1941 she published her first book of short stories, *A Curtain of Green*, which drew on the hundreds of photographs she had taken. Many of her stories address racism, struggling with the origins of hatred and prejudice, and all of them are written with a sympathetic ear, a genuine love for her characters.

She stayed away from overtly addressing the national events going on around her, with one exception. The night that civil rights activist Medgar Evers was shot in his driveway right in her hometown, she wrote a story in a fit of anger called "Where Is the Voice Coming From" that tries to get inside the mind of a racist, psychopathic killer. It was published two months later in the *New Yorker*.

From there, she wrote seven books in fourteen years and took a hiatus of several more to care for her dying mother. Her grief and suffering found expression in her novel *The Optimist's Daughter*, which gained her the Pulitzer Prize for fiction.

Though she was originally pigeonholed as a "Southern writer" and regionalist, her mastery of language, strong observations of "each other's human plight" in all its tragic, hilarious, and glorious detail, and universal appeal have placed her firmly among the world's great storytellers.

◆◆◆◆◆◆◆◆◆◆◆◆◆

FURTHER READING

The Collected Stories of Eudora Welty (various editions)

A Curtain of Green (1941)

The Optimist's Daughter (1972)

One Writer's Beginnings (1984)

◆◆◆◆◆◆◆◆◆◆◆◆◆

The Double Life of a Diarist
ANAÏS NIN
1903–1977

——◆◆◆◆——

To Anaïs Nin, the bourgeois life was the equivalent of death, characterized by boredom, monotony, and complacency. She refused to be a desperate housewife. When a woman's life is defined by limitations, if she has a hungry spirit, she is going to try to find a way to feed it one way or another—by creating drama in real life or by writing about it. Nin did both, and she told all in her famous diaries. Privilege and security do not necessarily take away one's desire for a more fulfilling life. As she wrote, "I am aware of being in a beautiful prison, from which I can only escape by writing."

Angela Anaïs Juana Antolina Rosa Edelmira Nin y Culmell was born in France to Cuban parents. Her father was a concert pianist who abandoned the family when she was eleven, after which she and her mother immigrated to the United States. En route to her new home, Nin wrote a letter to her father, begging him to come back, but she never sent it. This letter was the beginning of her diary, which she would continue writing for the rest of her life and which eventually contained forty thousand pages.

Nin dropped out of high school to become an artist's model in order to help her mother pay the bills, but she continued reading extensively. In her late twenties she married banker Hugh Guiler (also known as Ian Hugo) and they moved to Paris, where she tried to become a conventional wife. That didn't work out so well. They decided to have an open marriage, and so Nin was a demure housewife on the one hand and a polyamorous bohemian writer on the other. This persona of free-spirited writer was carefully crafted, a sort of dream of what it meant to live like an artist, and in her diaries, Hugo is conveniently absent.

In 1931, she met the writer Henry Miller, and they got involved in a years-long passionate love affair, throughout which Nin supported him, renting him a Paris apartment and financing the publication of *Tropic of Cancer*. The two of them, along with other avant-garde writers, started their own publishing company, Siana

Editions, publishing literature that no other publishers would touch because it was considered obscene. Much of what we know about Miller's (and his wife June's) personal life comes from Nin's diaries—and their love letters are real scorchers.

This need to write was for me as strong as the need to live . . . It was a second life, it was my way of living in a more heightened way.

In 1939 Anaïs and Hugo moved to the United States to escape the war. She underwent psychoanalysis, in which she dealt with her issues surrounding her father. She hung out with the Beat poets, experimented with LSD, and had relationships with many high-profile men, among them John Steinbeck, Edmund Wilson, and James Agee. She struggled to get her work published and eventually bought her own printing press in order to get her books out into the world—now that's one (expensive) way to self-publish. The sales of her novels weren't strong, and she was constantly frustrated by her lack of success.

She met a gorgeous young park ranger named Rupert Pole and began living a secret bigamist, bicoastal life, marrying Pole (despite still being married to Hugo!) and spending half her time in New York and half her time in Los Angeles, pretending this was travel for work.

It wasn't until 1966 that *The Diary of Anaïs Nin* was first published. Reviewed on the front page of the *New York Times Book Review* to great praise, it was an immediate success. Despite claiming to not be a women's libber, Nin became a feminist icon and started traveling around the world as a celebrity lecturer. Finally, there was demand for her work, and all seven volumes of her diaries were published. Her introspective and deeply personal writing struck a chord with women at a time when sexual liberation and self-actualization were becoming hot topics, and it still resonates today.

FURTHER READING

The Diary of Anaïs Nin, volumes 1—7 (1969—81)

Delta of Venus (1977)

Little Birds (1979)

Henry and June (1986)

Lonely Heart

CARSON McCULLERS

1917–1967

————✦✦✦✦————

L ula Carson Smith was a child prodigy, but not of writing: she started playing piano as soon as one arrived in her house when she was ten. She could play a song perfectly after hearing it only once or twice, and she practiced for hours every day. Born in Columbus, Georgia, to a jewelry store owner and a housewife, she preferred playing piano to her schoolwork. Her mother dreamed Lula would become a concert pianist, but misdiagnosed and untreated rheumatic fever left the young girl bedridden and without stamina. Books became her comfort, and she began to write. Not surprisingly, as an oddball herself (a sickly recluse who started wearing only boys' clothes), her characters were a menagerie of misfits.

> I live with the people I create and it has always
> made my essential loneliness less keen.

———

She left for New York when she was seventeen, supposedly to study piano at Juilliard, but she ended up at Columbia and New York Universities, studying creative writing instead. Going back and forth between home in Georgia and New York, depending on her health, she married James Reeves McCullers Jr., whom she met on an army base near her hometown. She also started writing her first novel, *The Heart Is a Lonely Hunter*. Houghton Mifflin gave her a $500 contract and published it when she was just twenty-three. Critics praised the book for its maturity and themes of loneliness and isolation. The book caused a sensation, and she became the toast of the town. The *New York Times* would write in her obituary that the book "paved the way for what became the American Southern gothic genre."

Her marriage was rocky, to say the least. They were both bisexual and separated when they each fell in love with the composer David Diamond, which became the basis of the love triangles in *The Ballad of the Sad Café* and *The Member of the Wedding*.

While on a break from her marriage, McCullers moved in with poet W. H. Auden in Brooklyn, and they rented an apartment from the literature editor at *Harper's*, where they befriended a diverse band of celebrities and writers, among them Tennessee Williams, Truman Capote, Christopher Isherwood, Gypsy Rose Lee, Salvador Dalí, and Richard Wright. Smoking three packs of cigarettes a day and drinking excessively, she also wrote constantly.

McCullers won a fellowship grant and started working on *The Member of the Wedding*, but between her illnesses and the book being described by her as a "holy terror," it took her five years to write and didn't live up to her debut. Being of unsound mind and body, she ended up with a nervous breakdown and lung problems (three packs a day!), at which point her husband, Reeves, came back to take care of her, although he also struggled with his own issues and was deeply disillusioned with the marriage and his own failed writing career. After World War II they lived in Paris, where at one point he tried to convince her they should die by suicide together. She feared for her life and fled to the United States; he followed through on his mission, killing himself in a hotel room.

Her five novels, two plays, short stories, children's book, nonfiction essays, and poems covered the injustices of segregation, alcoholism, blind conformity, the apathy of the masses, and desolation. In the last years of her life she suffered from breast cancer and several cerebral strokes, which paralyzed her on one side, before dying from one final stroke. At the time she was at work on her autobiography, *Illumination and the Night Glare*, an unfinished work that was eventually published thirty years after her death, in recognition of her role as one of the most talented writers of her generation. McCullers's was a completely fresh, if dark, voice that identified isolation as a painful aspect of the human condition, what she called "the malady."

FURTHER READING

The Heart Is a Lonely Hunter (1940)

The Member of the Wedding (1946)

The Ballad of the Sad Café (1951)

A Free Woman

DORIS LESSING

1919–2013

—— ✦✦✦✦ ——

Doris Lessing is a tough lady to nail down. Independent and contrarian, she lived through both World Wars, Nazism, the Great Depression, the Cold War, the threat of nuclear annihilation, genocide, apartheid, the rise of technology, the fall of the British Empire, and the women's movement. She was on a serpentine journey of constant reinvention as she fell in love and wrestled with her ideals through her writing. Her subjects are vast: racial inequality, colonialism, the difficult relationships between men and women, the inner landscape of psychology and mental breakdown, politics, utopian societies, and survivalism.

Welcome to the twentieth century.

Lessing has been labeled a feminist writer, a Communist writer, a mystic, a psychological writer, a science fiction writer, and a prophet. On the one hand, John Leonard, a book critic for the *New York Times*, described her as "one of the half-dozen most interesting minds to have chosen to write fiction in English in this century." On the other hand, readers and critics sometimes have become frustrated at her constant literary experimentation. She herself felt that "a writer is the conscience of the world."

Her writing is so varied but can be understood as the result of three periods when she became deeply committed to specific ideologies: first, Communism; then radical psychiatry; and finally Sufism, Taoism, and personal and cosmic evolution.

She was born Doris Tayler in what was then Persia, now Iran. Her father was a British captain during World War I and met her mother when she nursed him after his leg was amputated. He worked at the Imperial Bank of Prussia, eventually answering the call (and subsequently failing) to make a fortune farming maize in the British colony of Southern Rhodesia (now Zimbabwe). The war loomed large in the family's household, and Doris heard much talk of the trenches and trauma. They weren't allowed to mix with the Africans, and her Edwardian mother was determined to raise a proper daughter, sending her to an awful convent school that young Doris escaped from when she was fourteen. That was the end of her formal education, but she became self-educated, reading the books her mother ordered from England: *The Secret Garden*, biblical tales, Rudyard Kipling, history books about Napoleon, the Crusades, and Benjamin Franklin, as well as Dickens, Scott, Stevenson, Kipling, D. H. Lawrence, Stendhal, Tolstoy, and Dostoevsky. She wrote throughout her childhood and later claimed that reading saved her.

You can only learn to be a better writer by actually writing.

Doris ran away to Salisbury, the capital, got married young, and had two babies. After four years, feeling stifled by the pressures of being the perfect housewife, she left her husband and children and joined the Left Book Club, a group of Communists, because they shared her love of reading. The head of the group, a German-Jewish refugee, Gottfried Lessing, became her second husband and they had a son. She divorced him, too, after four years but kept his last name. She said that she didn't have the proper skills for marriage and reflected, "There is a whole generation of women and it was as if their lives came to a stop when they had children. Most of them got pretty neurotic—because, I think, of the contrast between what they were taught at school they were capable of being and what actually happened to them." She often explored the dichotomy between motherhood and having an erotic life.

Her first novel, *The Grass Is Singing*, was well received, telling the story of a white woman and her complicated relationship with her black servant in South Africa. In 1956, she was declared a prohibited alien in both Southern Rhodesia and South Africa because of her outspokenness against colonialism and apartheid.

She moved to London, where she became a target of MI5, the internal affairs unit of the British Secret Service (James Bond worked for MI6, the terrorist unit). British spies tracked her every move, opened her mail, and stole manuscripts of hers for almost fifteen years.

In 1962, she released *The Golden Notebook*, her most famous and influential work, which sold millions of copies and established her as a major literary voice. The main character is a writer, Anna Wulf, a divorced single mother who is in creative crisis and on the verge of a nervous breakdown. The book has an unusual structure: It is comprised of Anna's five notebooks. The black notebook takes place in South

Africa, the red one focuses on her Communist activities, the yellow one is full of ideas for her writing, the blue details her day-to-day life, and in the fifth, the golden notebook, she tries to tie all her selves together. There's also a doomed love affair in which Anna expresses the inadequacies of (most) men in a frank sexual language that hadn't been heard in quite this way before. Women the world over read the book, and it became iconic of the feminist movement, although Lessing denies that was her intention.

Her political beliefs and her honest depictions of women's anger, resentment, and disillusionment with men drew attacks from critics (how predictable!), who called her "unfeminine." Siriol Hugh-Jones wrote in *Vogue* (a magazine for women!) that *The Golden Notebook* was "dismal, drab, embarrassing, sodden with a particularly useless form of self-pity . . . the sort of book which seriously sets the tide of female emancipation, if you care about the thing at all, back a good long way" and accused her character of trying "to live with the freedom of a man." (God forbid.) Lessing responded: "Apparently what many women were thinking, feeling, experiencing came as a great surprise." She says she was only trying to create a "map of the human mind," and it was from a female perspective because she was, obviously, a woman.

Later in life, after writing more than fifty books and inciting the world with her provocative questions, the honors and awards came to her at a rapid pace. Lessing was awarded the Nobel Prize for Literature in 2007. She turned down becoming a dame of the British Empire because, as she said, "There is no British Empire." Margaret Atwood wrote an obituary in which she called Lessing "fearless" and said, "If there were a Mount Rushmore of 20th Century writers, Doris Lessing would most certainly be carved upon it" (probably right next to the carving of Atwood herself).

FURTHER READING

The Grass Is Singing (1950)

The Golden Notebook (1962)

Under My Skin: Volume One of My Autobiography, to 1949 (1962)

Walking in the Shade: Volume Two of My Autobiography, 1949–1962 (1998)

CLARICE LISPECTOR

1920–1977

B eautiful, glamorous, brilliant, and enigmatic, Clarice Lispector garnered a cult following of fans who simply call her "Clarice." Strange, disconcerting, and challenging, her texts bend the rules of fiction. Her avant-garde, stream-of-consciousness work takes risks and requires patience. She has been called a "literary magician," a "female Chekhov on the beaches of Guanabara," and a sorceress of sorts. Her mystical, mythical legacy is just now being rediscovered, thanks in great part to Benjamin Moser's 2009 biography of her, *Why This World*, in which he calls her "a caster of spells, literally enchanting, her nervous ghost haunting every branch of the Brazilian arts." Fortunately, at this point in history, being called a witch is a compliment (and doesn't involve being burned at the stake).

Born Chaya Pinkhasovna in the Ukraine to a Jewish family suffering through post–World War I pogroms, Clarice emigrated with her family after her grandfather was murdered and her mother was raped. In Brazil, her brilliant father found himself penniless and a widower when Clarice was just nine. Despite this, he put everything into educating his daughters, and Clarice eventually ended up studying law at the elite National Law Faculty at the University of Brazil, where she was the only Jew and one of just three women. She sought justice for prisoners and later became a rising fashion journalist, got married, and published her first novel, *Near to the Wild Heart*, at twenty-three.

It became an immediate phenomenon. A journalist described the impact of her book: "We have no memory of a more sensational debut, which lifted to such prominence a name that, until shortly before, had been completely unknown."

Her entire body of work is one extended autobiography of a woman and her development as an artist. Her books don't have a traditional plot but are more philosophical works about existential crisis.

Shortly after her first work came out, she moved overseas in support of her husband's work as a diplomat, spending two decades outside of Brazil in Switzerland, Italy, England, and Washington, D.C. Being a diplomat's wife bored her to tears, and Lispector became depressed and created two Clarices. The first was the brilliant artist and writer; the second, a middle-class housewife, and it was within that clash of selves that she wrote. As a bourgeois wife who gave up her career as a journalist, and a mother who gave birth to a schizophrenic son, she turned her experiences into art.

I think that when I'm not writing I'm dead.

Benjamin Moser says it is the influence of the Kabbalists, Jewish mystics to whom her father introduced her, that informed her abstract prose and her unusual—or total lack of—grammar. Poor grammar becomes a symbol of her characters' distress or instability or transformation rather than a symptom of her lack of fluency in her second language, the one she wrote in, Portuguese.

One of Lispector's most recurring and distinctive images is cockroaches. In *The Passion According to G.H.*, the narrator crushes a cockroach and then eats it. In another story the narrator complains that cockroaches appear every night in her apartment like "evil secrets," and she comes up with a recipe to kill them. Cockroaches—and existentialism—may partially explain why she is so often compared to Kafka.

Her second book, *The Chandelier*, didn't sell well, and her third manuscript, *Love in a Besieged City*, had a hard time finding a publisher. When it was finally released, the critics considered it difficult to read and a real head-scratcher. Despondent, she didn't publish another novel for twelve years. She was also badly burned in her bed after falling asleep with a cigarette, after which she became even more of a recluse.

Lispector was only too aware of how women had been silenced throughout history, and her characters reflect that. What does it mean to be a poet, an artist, stuck in a beautiful woman's body, full of feminist ideals and brilliance, and to succeed wildly at such a young age (her debut was called "the greatest novel a woman has ever written in the Portuguese language"), only to then live the dull life of a diplomat's wife struggling to get her new work out into the world?

But Lispector was determined to "see it to the end" and never stopped writing or persevering, and, after writing eighty-five novels and short stories, she is finally getting her due. In Brazil, where there is a national obsession with what she called her "anti-literature," her books are sold from vending machines in subway stations. Her avant-garde work is just now being translated and read in English, continuing to grow her cult following.

◆◆◆◆◆◆◆◆◆◆◆◆◆

FURTHER READING

The Besieged City

The Chandelier

The Complete Stories

Near to the Wild Heart

A Breath of Life

The Passion According to G.H.

The Hour of the Star

Água Viva

Why This World: A Biography of Clarice Lispector, by Benjamin Moser (2009)

◆◆◆◆◆◆◆◆◆◆◆◆◆

Tragic Glamour

EILEEN CHANG

(Chang Ai-ling)

1920–1995

—◆◆◆◆—

All a writer can strive for is to live with integrity. A real writer
can only really write about what he himself thinks. What a
writer should or should not write is ultimately beside the point.

———

She cut a glamorous figure, capturing a time in history before the Cultural Revolution, becoming a symbol of Shanghai art deco glamour. She survived the Japanese invasion of China during World War II and was one of China's most celebrated writers in her time. Tragically, with the rise of Mao, Eileen Chang was forced to leave her country, her work disappeared for decades, and she never quite received the international renown she deserved in her lifetime.

Chang was born in Shanghai to aristocratic parents, who divorced when she was just five, after her father took on a concubine. Her socialite mother ran off to ski in the Alps (with bound feet!), and Eileen was stuck with her opium-addicted father, who would beat her and once locked her in her room for six months. After that she ran away, publishing an account of her experiences in the *Shanghai Evening Post*.

Chang studied literature at the University of Hong Kong until the Japanese attacked the city in 1941, forcing her to return home, where she published her first stories and novels.

Her work found a devoted following and she became a popular literary star, her characters often dark, dissolute, and tragic. However, her work was often dismissed as "bourgeois," too wrapped up in trivialities at a time when male politics took center stage.

Rail thin, she dressed glamorously. She used the first money she made, when she was barely a teenager—by publishing a cartoon in the local newspaper—to buy a tube of lipstick. When she first started to become known as a writer, she was also building her own business designing clothes.

Chang's sense of style, inherited from her mother, showed up in spades in her writing. You could say she suffered from sensual, sensory overload. Through colors, smells, sounds, and bitter humor, this sensibility comes through in the vivid details of her writing: the stench of opium; women so thin their jade bracelets go up to their elbows; dresses "the color of chopped beef"; life described as an "extravagant gown covered with lice"; feeling like a "bird embroidered onto a screen . . . in clouds of gold stitched onto a screen of melancholy satin."

Chang made fun of the upper class's consumerism, classism, decadence, and drug addiction, and also wrote sympathetically about the common person, women experiencing oppression, poverty, and abortion, and orphans dying in the streets. She was criticized as "apolitical" for writing both anti-Communist literature and satires of her own privileged class. She refused to take sides, focusing instead on something a little less transient: how the powerful (men) influence the lives of the powerless (women).

Of course, all of this exquisite detail of haute couture and jade jewelry, sex and betrayal, jealousies, femme fatales, painting, music, fashion, and literature made her nonthreatening at a time when Communism was on the rise. That is, until she worked as a translator of Hemingway and Emerson (she had studied English) for the United States Information Services. Her work there led to commissioned anti-Communist writing, including her novels *Rice Sprout Song* and *The Naked Earth*. When Mao took power, there was a target on her back, and her work was banned in China. She escaped to the United States and ignored the many prominent editors who tried to publish her.

Ang Lee, who created the 2008 film *Lust, Caution* based on a story that took Chang twenty years to write, called her a "fallen angel" of Chinese literature. In the 1990s she was rediscovered through pirated copies of her work, and she is now considered one of the top mainland Chinese authors. When *Small Reunions* (written in 1976) was released in China in 2009, it sold more than a million copies. Her works are just now being studied at American universities, earning more of the recognition they deserve.

FURTHER READING

Love in a Fallen City, translated by Karen S. Kingsbury (2006)

Little Reunions, translated by Martin Merz and Jane Weizhen Pan (2018)

Liberator of Language Barriers
ROSARIO CASTELLANOS
1925–1974

━━━◆◆◆◆◆━━━

[No one,] not even myself, considered literature a
profession a woman could practice. It was thought to
be an activity no rational person would choose.

———

It's hard to imagine, but in the early 1970s in Mexico, women were still considered innately inferior to men. *Innately*. It took the daughter of a wealthy coffee plantation owner who grew up in the southern Mexican state of Chiapas on the Guatemalan border to gain greater awareness for the idea that the subjugation of women was a social construct, not God's will. In Rosario Castellanos's 1971 speech "Self Denial: A Crazy Virtue," presented to President Luis Echeverria at Mexico's National Museum of Anthropology and History, she boldly spoke of how women, despite earning the vote, still suffered restricted access to higher education, professional opportunities, and salary equity. She encouraged women to beautify themselves not with fashion, hair, makeup, or high heels, which she called "an instrument of daily torture, which limited the mobility of women," but with knowledge. Not bad advice, then or now. She was called "the intellectual starting point for the liberation of Mexican women" by journalist Elena Poniatowska.

Growing up a child of privilege, Rosario was cared for by a Mayan woman and a girl her own age who were paid to be her caregiver and companion, respectively. Through them she came to understand the Mayan language, Tzotzil, and Mayan prayers and legends, as well as to appreciate the problems that language barriers can create and the injustice inherent in the lives of the indigenous people in Mexico, particularly women, who did not have a voice. At this point the laws and constitution had not been translated into Tzotzil.

Years later she would personally translate the Mexican constitution. Working with the Chiapas Institute of Sciences and the Arts and Mexico's Instituto Nacional

Indigenista, she became the director of the UNAM Information and Press Office, providing media in indigenous languages to Native communities and promoting literacy.

Her family's circumstances changed from wealthy aristocratic landowners to middle-class city dwellers as a result of land reforms. They moved to Mexico City, and Castellanos wrote that this "destroyed the certainty of my racial, social, and economic superiority," making her "seek alternatives, values to conquer and make my own in order to feel worthy of living." She eventually gave up her inherited land to the people who worked on it.

She went on to study philosophy and became a part of the Generation of 1950, a group of intellectuals, at the National Autonomous University of Mexico (NAUM). Traveling through Europe with Dolores Castro, eventually studying linguistics in Madrid, gave her a new perspective on her identity, and she became influenced by the European feminist writers she encountered, such as Simone de Beauvoir, Simone Weil, Gabriela Mistral, and Virginia Woolf.

Her greatest and best-known work is the Chiapanecan Trilogy, written with help of a Rockefeller Foundation fellowship, which brought her international acclaim. In all three books, she looked at the difficulties of marginalized, subordinated people, particularly indigenous people and women. Her semiautobiographical books *The Nine Guardians*, *The Book of Lamentations*, and *Royal City* were mystical, fictional imaginings of a Mayan uprising taking place in the present and looked at the nature of oppression and all its horrors.

When she was in her mid-forties, Castellanos was appointed Mexico's ambassador to Israel and moved to Tel Aviv. She died there, of accidental electrocution in her embassy apartment, at age forty-nine. Prime Minister Golda Meir called her "one of the most brilliant minds I have ever met."

FURTHER READING

A Rosario Castellanos Reader: An Anthology of Her Poetry, Short Fiction, Essays, and Drama, edited and translated by Maureen Ahern (1988)

The Nine Guardians, translated by Irene Nicholson (1960)

The Book of Lamentations, translated by Ester Allen (1996; originally published in 1962 in Spanish)

FLANNERY O'CONNOR

1925–1964

A nice Catholic girl and true believer, Flannery O'Connor constantly struggled in her soul between her desire to be a great writer and her desire to remain devout, what she called the "stinking mad shadow of Jesus." She was deadly serious in her pursuit of excellence in art and faith, and she was scathing in her criticism of mediocrity and the trivial.

Flannery was born in Savannah, Georgia, to a prominent Irish Catholic family in the evangelical Protestant Bible Belt, and her work was influenced by the places she lived, the people around her, her undeniable intellect and deep faith, and her battle with lupus, a disease her father also had and from which he died when she was just fifteen.

> I think it's better to begin with the story, and then you know you've got something. Because the theme is more or less something that's in you, but if you intellectualize it too much you probably destroy your novel.

In high school, she was a cartoonist, submitting to significant publications like the *New Yorker* (hey, she had high standards) and collecting rejection slips, as well as writing poems and drawing cartoons for the local newspaper, the *Corinthian*. Her talent gained her a scholarship to the Iowa Writers' Workshop, but she felt like she stuck out like a sore thumb, earnest in her soul-searching in a way her secular peers were not, suffering as they were from "intellectual quackery."

While in Iowa, O'Connor started writing a journal addressed to God, a collection of prayers and meditations that make a strong argument for the connection between spirituality and creativity. In what became *A Prayer Journal*, she wrote, "Dear God, tonight it is not disappointing because you have given me a story. Don't let me ever think, dear God, that I was anything but the instrument for Your story—just like the typewriter was mine."

Through her journaling, she came to see her artistic vocation as a gift, and when she turned to fiction, her characters became her spiritual doppelgängers, quite different from herself in appearances, but suffering from their own demons. She saw the human race as "fallen" and living in a wasteland of rationalism and technology, and she used satire and black humor to show stark spiritual quests and our need to find redemption.

O'Connor wrote her first novel at the famous artists' retreat Yaddo. Her time there was productive, although she didn't exactly fit in with the hard-drinking, religiously conflicted others (Robert Lowell, Patricia Highsmith). She refused to join them on their benders and was considered eccentric and a little too fanatical. No matter; *Wise Blood*, the dark work she wrote there, won her the Rinehart-Iowa Fiction award. William Faulkner said of it, "Now that's good stuff." High praise, indeed.

She wrote works that showed a highly developed ear for Southern dialect, sharp wit, a strong sense of irony, and an unrelenting forceful spiritual vision, focusing on original sin, guilt, and the need for grace. In her most famous works—the short story collection *A Good Man Is Hard to Find*, her second novel, *The Violent Bear It Away*, and the posthumously published collection of short stories *Everything That Rises Must Converge*—she writes about convicts, murderers, racism, prejudices, judgment, and how we assume moral, spiritual, or social superiority over others based on our own narrow-mindedness. *A Good Man Is Hard to Find* was modeled on Dante's *Purgatory*, as "nine stories about original sin, with my compliments."

O'Connor's often physically disfigured and grotesque characters were misfits and homicidal maniacs, hell-bent on revenge, full of rage. There was a lot of matricide (which doesn't speak well of her relationship with her mother). Her art was a way for O'Connor to express her moral vision. And, yes, she was judgy. But she wrote about sin and grace in the modern world with a dash of humor, a heavy dose of violence, and a sprinkling of salvation.

O'Connor watched the world becoming more secular and asked us all to be better and reach for a more meaningful experience and a higher state of consciousness, as she strove to do. It may seem a little too high-minded, but have you looked at your Instagram feed lately? Maybe she was on to something.

O'Connor died from lupus at age thirty-nine, after living at Andalusia, a family farm, with her mother. She called her disease the "Red Wolf" and wrote about it with her signature dark humor. While physically deteriorating, she continued to write and found great pleasure in tending to her forty peacocks.

The Complete Stories was first published in 1971, seven years after her death, and she received the National Book Award. It was the first time the award was given posthumously. The panel of judges unanimously voted to waive the rule that no author dead more than two years could win. She was *that* good.

✦ ✦ ✦ ✦ ✦ ✦ ✦ ✦ ✦ ✦ ✦ ✦ ✦

FURTHER READING

A Good Man Is Hard to Find (1955)

The Violent Bear It Away (1960)

Everything That Rises Must Converge (1965)

The Complete Stories (1971)

✦ ✦ ✦ ✦ ✦ ✦ ✦ ✦ ✦ ✦ ✦ ✦ ✦

NELLE HARPER LEE

1926–2016

——◆◆◆◆——

H arper Lee is as famous for having (almost) never written another book as she is for writing her game-changer about racial tensions and a small-town lawyer in Depression-era Alabama, *To Kill a Mockingbird*. She was also famously cranky and vigilant in maintaining her privacy, refusing to do interviews or even be quoted in the press, communicating only through her literary agency.

She won the Pulitzer Prize for fiction in 1961, and the film based on her book, starring Gregory Peck as the principled Atticus Finch, won several Academy Awards, but she told the *Mobile Register* that all she wanted was to disappear. She was—forgive me—an odd bird.

And can you really blame her for trying to maintain her privacy when her hometown had exploited her success, becoming a commercialized trinket- and T-shirt-selling Mockingbird museum (they even sold "Inspirational Writer's Water"), with vans full of tourists lingering in front of her house?

Lee grew up in Monroeville, Alabama. While her father was a lawyer and ran the local newspaper, her mother suffered from mental illness and rarely left the house. In kindergarten Nelle became best friends with her neighbor Truman Capote, who inspired her character Dill. They were two peas in a pod: passionate readers and aspiring writers, with difficult family lives—a "sissy" and a tomboy who defended him. It was Lee who wrote the profile of him for the Book of the Month Club newsletter when they chose *In Cold Blood* as their January 1966 selection. She also did research, reporting, and even some writing for it, although Capote never acknowledged her extensive contributions. She would later say of her and Capote's lifelong friendship and collaborations that they were "bound by a common anguish." Their heavy drinking was both the result of and a contributor to that anguish.

Her agent and friends said Lee was always writing, and rumors swirled of a true-crime manuscript called *The Reverend*, about a preacher suspected of being a serial killer, but it never surfaced. There were also dubious claims of a manuscript being stolen, and manuscripts that were destroyed: Lee once told a New York City neighbor, "I just threw three hundred pages of a manuscript down the incinerator."

> *Any writer worth [her] salt writes to please [her]self . . . an exorcism of not necessarily [her] demon, but of [her] divine discontent.*

———

Her masterpiece made her wildly wealthy, but Miss Nelle never took to the material trappings of success. She lived on the Upper East Side of New York in a small, rent-controlled apartment. In her hometown she stayed with her sister in a small brick house. The *New York Times* painted a bleak picture of her frugal later life, saying that she was "seen around town in sweatpants looking for bargains at a Dollar General Store, washing her clothes at a local Laundromat, drinking coffee at a McDonald's."

She was eighty-eight and in an assisted living home after a stroke when *Go Set a Watchman* was published. A high-profile copyright suit followed, in which Lee's lawyers claimed that she had been tricked into having it published. It was the best-selling book of 2015, considered by some to be a long-awaited sequel to her hit from decades earlier, though many others pointed out that it actually appeared to be a rough draft of that same novel. Written (and abandoned) in the 1950s, before the manuscript that would become *Mockingbird*, the book portrays Atticus Finch as a racist and segregationist—far from the character millions of readers knew and admired.

Since 1960, *To Kill a Mockingbird* has been translated into more than forty languages and sold more than forty million copies worldwide, and it is required reading in many schools, still selling more than a million copies a year. In 2018, famous screenwriter and playwright Aaron Sorkin adapted the book into a successful Broadway play. One-hit (or perhaps two-hit) wonder or not, *Mockingbird* is an important book that opened the eyes of millions of people to a difficult time in the American South's history.

FURTHER READING

To Kill a Mockingbird (1960)

Go Set a Watchman (2015)

MAYA ANGELOU

1928–2014

———— ◆◆◆◆ ————

Some critics review my work by saying, "Maya Angelou is a natural writer." Being a natural writer is much like being a natural open-heart surgeon.

————

Maya Angelou was a true Renaissance woman over the course of her long and fruitful life, at one time or another a streetcar conductor, madam (!), cook, waitress, civil rights activist, dancer, actress, playwright, and director. And, of course, poet and writer. She won three Grammys for her spoken-word albums, was nominated for a Tony Award for her role in the 1972 play *Look Away*, and toured Europe in *Porgy and Bess*. She accompanied Martin Luther King Jr. at his New York City speeches as the coordinator for the Southern Christian Leadership Conference. She recited a poem she wrote for the occasion at Bill Clinton's inauguration and was awarded the Presidential Medal of Freedom. Oprah Winfrey called her one of her most important teachers, "my mentor, mother/sister and friend." But she will be remembered best for her eloquent, powerful writing.

And she worked hard at it. She loved the sound of the English language and said it took her forever to make her words sing.

She was born Marguerite Annie Johnson in St. Louis, Missouri, and was sent with her brother by train when she was three to live with her father's mother in Stamps, Arkansas, after her parents split up. At seven years old, she was raped by her mother's boyfriend, and when she told her family about it, her uncles killed him. This experience was profoundly formative: She saw the power of her own voice, and the consequences of using it. She had learned her voice could kill people, and as a result didn't speak for the next six years. Her grandmother tied a pencil with string to a little notebook for her and she carried it everywhere, using notes to communicate. She learned to listen and observe very carefully and said, "I used to think I could make my whole body an ear. I've listened so assiduously, and out of that came the love of language."

After having a child and leaving home at seventeen, Angelou began her wide array of careers. She joined the Harlem Writer's Guild in the late 1950s and became close with James Baldwin, who encouraged her writing. She worked for newspapers while living in Cairo and then Ghana, where she fought apartheid and wrote the first screenplay to be produced by an African American woman, *Georgia, Georgia*.

In 1970 she published the first book in a seven-volume autobiography, *I Know Why the Caged Bird Sings*. In it, she wrote about her childhood and how the power of words and ideas from great writers helped form and save her. Now a beloved classic, it was an international sensation when it came out, praised for its brutal honesty. That same honesty also resulted in the book being banned for its sexual assault scene. It takes courage to speak the truth. *I Know Why the Caged Bird Sings* is now read in schools all over the world.

Angelou eventually settled down to a professorship at Wake Forest University, where she stayed for the rest of her life. She has described her disparate lives and personas, her rich experiences, as working together like a patchwork quilt: "There are those who would like to think that their lives are long tapestries. The truth is that everybody's life is a matter of happenstance, mis-happenstance, intention and accident, courage and cowardice."

Six feet tall, bodacious, wise, and in-spiring, she left a powerful legacy with her poems (there is nothing quite like "Still I Rise" or "Phenomenal Woman") as well as her thirty-six books. After having accomplished so much and lived so fully, when asked what dreams she had left, she replied, "To write a sentence so gracious it slips off the page, that's it." Metaphorically, her words have done more than that and have flown off the page, touching the lives of people all over the world.

FURTHER READING

I Know Why the Caged Bird Sings (1969)

And Still I Rise (1978)

The Heart of a Woman (1981)

The Collected Autobiographies of Maya Angelou (2004)

The Complete Poetry (2015)

URSULA K. LE GUIN

1929–2018

U rsula K. Le Guin created a magical world with a school for wizards decades before J. K. Rowling did the same with Harry Potter. Her first book, *Earthsea*, follows protagonist Ged, who goes to the Roke School of Wizardry to learn the art of magic. Science fiction at that point was strictly pulp, male-centric, and marginalized in a society that looked down on the fantastical. Le Guin broke down the walls, saying that "every story must make its own rules."

She was a prolific world builder and called her books "thought experiments." She would draw detailed maps on large pieces of paper with crayon (she was raising three children at the time, and I guess that was the writing instrument closest to hand), creating fully thought-out names for places, cities, and rivers, and inventing entire languages. In *Earthsea* true mastery of something comes from knowing its name. In creating magic with words, Le Guin developed a parallel between wizards and writers.

Le Guin's father, Alfred Kroeber, was the head of the anthropology department at the University of California, Berkeley, and her mother was a writer. There were always books, music, and lots of stories and discussion in the household. There were also visitors from different backgrounds, among them exiled Jewish intellectuals who had fled Hitler and the last California Native Americans, who shared myths through their oral tradition. Ursula became very aware of culture, subculture, and the way societies are structured.

Le Guin said she never wanted to be a writer; she just always wrote, starting at age five. Her parents told her that when you are given a gift for something, it is your obligation to work at it, and that work is the most rewarding kind.

Educated at Radcliffe, she wrote for the college's literary magazine, but they wouldn't publish her stories. Realism was king. When she started sending her fantastical stories out, everyone commented on her gift for writing and storytelling, but no one knew what to do with her. When she finally sold a story to a pulp magazine for thirty dollars, it was a breakthrough. Her first five novels were all rejected, until Ace Books finally published *Rocannon's World*, an action-adventure story set in space with a man of science as her hero. She was thirty-seven.

She married historian Charles A. Le Guin in 1953, and they moved to Portland, Oregon. Her husband supported her work, and she supported his. She said she had a rule: "One person cannot do two fulltime jobs, but two persons can do three fulltime jobs—if they honestly share the work. The idea that you need an ivory tower to write in, that if you have babies you can't have books, that artists are somehow exempt from the dirty work of life—rubbish." She did her writing between 10 p.m. and midnight.

> *It was important to think about privilege and power and domination in terms of gender. Which was something that fantasy had not done.*

In her experimental, groundbreaking novel *The Left Hand of Darkness*, she invented a race of people who were androgynous and sexually active only once a month. They could choose to be a man or a woman—to be a father or to mother a child. It was her expedition into human cooperation, a look at moral dilemmas that explored what a world without class, racism, hierarchy, or inequality would look like. Throughout her career, she consciously chose to make most of her characters people of color. She invented "anarchist utopias." Taoist, Buddhist, and pacifist philosophies run deep in her work. Her stories have complicated characters with vices and virtues and strong inner lives who in their conflicted natures show a "spiritual journey and the struggles of good and evil in the soul."

She told the *Paris Review* that she didn't consider herself a science fiction writer; she considered herself a novelist and a poet and told them not to "shove me into your damn pigeonhole."

When she was finally welcomed into the canon at the National Book Awards in 2014 with a Lifetime Achievement Award, her speech caused quite a stir. Le Guin said she didn't want to see "American literature sold down the river" by the profit motive of the publishing industry and added, "Books aren't just commodities. Resistance and change often begin in art." She said this in a room full of people from the publishing industry.

Outspoken until the end, throughout her life, she never stopped telling her truth, writing twenty-one novels, eleven volumes of short stories, four collections of essays, twelve children's books, and six volumes of poetry. She took the then marginalized genres of fantasy and science fiction, completely disrupted them, and then elevated them to the status of literature.

＊＊＊＊＊＊＊＊＊＊＊＊＊＊

FURTHER READING

A Wizard of Earthsea (1968)

The Left Hand of Darkness (1969)

Lathe of Heaven (1971)

The Dispossessed (1974)

Dancing at the Edge of the World (1989)

＊＊＊＊＊＊＊＊＊＊＊＊＊＊

ROOMS OF THEIR OWN

Virginia Woolf laid out her views pretty clearly in *A Room of One's Own*, the book-length essay based on the lectures on Women and Fiction that she gave at two colleges in 1928: "A woman must have money and a room of her own if she is to write fiction." She could afford to be an idealist, but for the rest of us, a quiet place to work without distractions is difficult to come by (and money is an entirely separate matter). So how did Woolf and other female writers create their own writing spaces?

VIRGINIA WOOLF'S WRITING LODGE

When Virginia and Leonard Woolf bought Monk's House in the Sussex countryside, she turned a wooden toolshed in the garden into her writer's space. In the summer she had the brightness of the sun coming through large windows and stunning views. Unfortunately, in the winter, it would be so cold she could barely hold a pen, and eventually she would have to move to the main house. She wrote *Mrs. Dalloway* here, as well as many of her reviews, essays, and other correspondence, including her suicide note to Leonard.

J. K. ROWLING'S CAFÉ

—◆◆◆—

When J. K. Rowling was a new mother living on welfare, she began writing the Harry Potter books in the Elephant House café in Edinburgh while her baby was napping. Cut to her writing the final book in the series years later, surrounded by distractions and unable to work. She checked into the Balmoral Hotel, also in Edinburgh, and, after one extremely productive day there, moved in for an entire month to complete the book.

TONI MORRISON'S COUCH

—◆◆◆—

As a hardworking book editor and single mother of two boys, Morrison would get up early and write before she went to work. Here is her 1970s living room, where she would write, sitting on the couch, in the wee hours.

JANE AUSTEN'S MINIATURE DESK

It was on this tiny, twelves-ided walnut table at Chawton Cottage that Jane revised both *Sense and Sensibility* and *Pride and Prejudice* and did a majority of her later work. The other women in the house gave Jane her solitude and time to write, taking on most of the house and garden work, so she could devote herself to what would eventually become her internationally renowned and beloved novels.

MAYA ANGELOU'S HOTEL ROOM

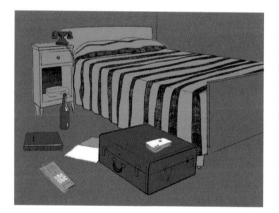

Angelou kept a hotel room in whichever town she lived, getting there at six-thirty in the morning and working until early afternoon. She never slept there but would lie down on the bed with "a bottle of sherry, a dictionary, *Roget's Thesaurus*, yellow pads, an ashtray, and a Bible." Then she'd go elsewhere and try to live like a normal person until the evening, when she would go back to her hotel room and read what she had written that morning and mark it up.

THE BRONTËS' PARLOR

◆◆◆

Crimson-upholstered furniture, books, and a warm fireplace give this room in Haworth Parsonage a cozy feel, but it is also a space full of creativity, passion, melancholy, and loss. The portrait of Charlotte hanging here was commissioned by her publisher after she became a huge success. The three sisters would write at the large dining table and walk around the room discussing their work. It is also said that Emily, having become too weak to walk, died on the couch in this room. When Anne also died, this room became Charlotte's domain, where she edited her sisters' work and met with Mrs. Gaskell to discuss her biography.

Chronicler of the Black Experience
TONI MORRISON
1931–2019

———◆◆◆◆———

I n a *New York Times Book Review* interview, Henry Louis Gates Jr. asked Maya
Angelou, "What books would you recommend to someone who wants to know
more about American culture?" She answered, "Read Toni Morrison's novels in
chronological order."

When she was awarded the Pulitzer Prize for *Beloved* in 1993 for "visionary
force and poetic import," Morrison said, "My work requires me to think about how
free I can be as an African American woman writer in my genderized, sexualized,
wholly racialized world." She was asked time after time how she felt about being
called a black writer. She said she never tired of the label, just the question. She
was proud of her blackness and found great depth in it, not limitations. There were
stories and a point of view that was not being told, so she told them with her own
unique narrative style, based on the oral tradition she grew up with. She took the
historical and translated it into the personal, showing the black experience in intimate terms. She wanted slavery and its legacy to be not just described, but *felt*.

She was born Chloe Anthony Wofford in Lorain, Ohio, to a shipyard welder and
a mother who sang in the church choir whose families had moved north as part of
the Great Migration. The family lived in six apartments, including one that was set
on fire by the landlord when they couldn't pay the four-dollar-per-month rent.

She grew up with Southern black folklore, songs, and stories. As a young bookworm she read Tolstoy, Dostoevsky, Flaubert, Theodore Dreiser, Jane Austen, and
Richard Wright. She went to an integrated school and at twelve converted to Cathol-
icism, taking her baptismal name, Anthony. Her friends started calling her Toni.
Shortly thereafter a teacher from middle school sent a note home to her parents
saying, "You and your husband would be remiss in your duties if you do not see to
it that this child goes to college." Her father took a second job in order to be able
to pay for her education. I think it's safe to say that this effort paid off. Morrison

established an impressive academic career, with degrees from Howard and Cornell, high-profile teaching gigs, and a position as chair at Princeton University.

An editor at Random House for twenty years, she published books by Angela Davis and Muhammad Ali while doing her own writing early in the mornings and on weekends, in part to escape an unhappy marriage. She eventually divorced and continued to work, write, and raise her two children. As the head of her household, she fought for fair pay, telling her employer that her "little woman's raise" was too low and that she meant serious business.

> If there is a book that you want to read, but it hasn't
> been written yet, you must be the one to write it.

She joined a writing group, where she wrote a story based on a girl she knew as a child who had prayed for blue eyes because white, blue-eyed, and straight hair were then considered the standards of beauty. It evolved into her novel *The Bluest Eye*. Morrison says, "What was driving me to write was the silence—so many stories untold and unexamined. There was a wide vacuum in the literature." She was thirty-nine when it was published, to mixed reviews and minimal sales. At a moment when the "black is beautiful" movement was just getting off the ground, she may have simply been before her time. But she kept on writing. Her next novel, published four years later, *Sula*, was nominated for the National Book Award, landing Morrison on the cover of *Newsweek*. She was the first African American woman to be on the cover of a national magazine since Zora Neale Hurston.

So, to be clear, she was a single mother, raising two boys, working full-time as an editor of groundbreaking top writers, fighting for equal pay, and waking up before dawn to write. She had no role models, no understanding of what it meant to earn a living as a "writer." As a teacher, yes, as an editor, yes, but she "didn't personally know any other women writers who were successful; it looked very much like a male preserve. It [was] almost as if you needed permission to write."

Having blocks of time to write was a luxury Morrison never had. It was always catch as catch can. All with the odds stacked against her.

Her critics could be brutal. When she won the Nobel Prize in 1993, her combination of feminism and focus on black culture had *Middle Passage* author Charles Johnson saying that her win was "a triumph of political correctness." Critic Stanley

Crouch said, "I hope this prize inspires her to write better books." Despite this, Morrison was of course thrilled, and happy her mother was still alive to celebrate it with her.

As a writer, Morrison changed how stories were being told and knew how words could be used to heal and help shape society. She used hers in unusual and powerful ways. They clearly had a major impact, and her numerous awards and accolades—too many to list here—show she didn't just make a dent; she smashed the proverbial wall down.

FURTHER READING

The Bluest Eye (1970)

Sula (1973)

Song of Solomon (1977)

Tar Baby (1981)

Beloved (1987)

Jazz (1992)

The Source of Self-Regard: Selected Essays, Speeches, and Meditations (2019)

Telling Stories in Order to Live
JOAN DIDION
b. 1934

———◆◆◆◆———

If you were to see Joan Didion, slight and frail-looking, pretty and reticent, before reading her work, the blunt steeliness of her writing might surprise you at first. While appearing emotionally disconnected, she deliberately tells her reader of being in "acute emotional distress" and feeling that "writing is an irrelevant act." The reader witnesses events in the moment, as Didion documents them in her dispassionate tone. She pulls the reader in with that visceral experience alongside her genius prose. It is almost passive-aggressive.

Didion says that she writes in order to figure out what she feels and in order to make sense of what has happened. But, in New Journalism—of which she is one of the sole female practitioners—writing yourself as a narrator who is also a character is part of the game, as is dialogue, a unique point of view, and other novelistic qualities that make up "literary nonfiction." Didion became an icon—cool, chic, enigmatic—and helped define and make sense of a turbulent and disturbing era, writing about the seamy side of the late 1960s. A Californian at heart, "Joan made it ok to be serious about L.A.," as fellow writer and Californian Eve Babitz said.

Born and raised in Sacramento, she was an introverted child whose mother gave her a Big 5 notebook when she was five and told her to stop whining and write everything down. She used to copy Hemingway's sentences into her notebook to learn how they were constructed. She studied English at Berkeley, won the Prix de Paris essay contest, and went to New York to write at *Vogue*, where she worked for ten years. Her first piece, "Self Respect," made it onto the cover in August 1961. While she tended to write about things unusual for a fashion magazine, she says that it was at *Vogue* that she learned to write, her editor ruthless with a red pen. At night, because "that's what one did," she started writing her first novel, *River Run*, which was eventually published to little critical or popular acclaim.

In the meantime, she had met John Gregory Dunne, then working at *Time*, and they married. She said she had to marry another writer because anyone else would lose patience with her. They moved to L.A., started writing for magazines, got into the movie business, collaborating on scripts, and adopted a daughter, Quintana Roo. And they partied hard.

Quiet and prone to migraines, Joan saw her husband as her protector, the shield between her and the world. She once checked into a psychiatric clinic with severe vertigo and nausea; he took care of all the business. They were each other's best editors. There was nothing either one of them wrote that the other didn't read.

The only reader I hear is me. I am always writing to myself, so very possibly I'm committing an aggressive and hostile act toward myself.

Didion found a home at the *Saturday Evening Post*, where she published her groundbreaking and controversial essay about the alarming shifts of the strung-out counterculture, "Slouching Towards Bethlehem," which became the title of her 1968 collection of essays about California. She tells of meeting druggies, dropouts, runaways, lost souls, and kindergartners on LSD.

The book's publication made her a literary star. She was seen as a visionary, intuitive, and paranoid, almost clairvoyant about where the culture was going, and as a result she became a cultural phenomenon, with dedicated superfans and followers among readers as well as critics and the media. The *New York Times* called the book "a rich display of some of the best prose written today in this country."

Joan and John were part of the uber-hip, fabulous, booze- and drug-filled, celebrity-laden Hollywood social scene. In 1969, Didion completed her third book, *Play It as It Lays*, a novel about the shadowy side of sunny Hollywood. In 1971, they moved into a house just north of Malibu and began writing screenplays together, twenty in total, with mixed results. They said they were doing it for fun, glamour, and money; no serious writer would write for the movies in earnest. Didion has said that she didn't really consider it writing, more like "writing down notes for the director."

The White Album, her second essay collection, is mainly about L.A. during the years she and Dunne and Quintana lived in a house on Franklin Avenue in Hollywood at the end of the sixties.

Whether walking into hippie dens in Haight-Ashbury in 1967, moving among the death squads in El Salvador, or interviewing Linda Kasabian, disciple of Charles Manson and chief witness to the horrific murders of Sharon Tate and four others, she witnessed things that would be hard to stomach without developing a mindset of detachment.

Didion turned her focus to politics, critical essays, and memoir and started writing for the *New York Review of Books* and eventually the *New Yorker*.

Her most difficult work was also her most successful. On Christmas Eve, 2003, her daughter, Quintana, complained of flu-like symptoms and ended up in the hospital, which led to a series of complications that included pneumonia, septic shock, a coma, brain bleeding, and several surgeries. Joan's husband, devastated by his daughter's illness, died at the dinner table from a heart attack during her treatment. The loss was severe for Joan. *The Year of Magical Thinking*, which Lili Anolik described in *Vanity Fair* as a book about "loss and grief and pain transformed into meditations on loss and grief and pain; they're loss and grief and pain aestheticized," not only won the National Book Award, it sold well over one million copies.

Two months before the book's publication, Quintana died at age thirty-nine of acute pancreatitis after months in intensive care. In an effort to help Didion survive her grief and guilt, friend and playwright David Hare worked with her to bring *Magical Thinking* to Broadway, in the form of a monologue starring Vanessa Redgrave, who had also prematurely lost a daughter. Hare insisted Didion include Quintana in the monologue, which inspired her bestselling memoir *Blue Nights*.

Didion was always there to get the best story she could and attempted to make sense out of the chaos she saw. In her words, "We tell ourselves stories in order to live . . . We look for the sermon in the suicide, for the social or moral lesson in the murder of five. We interpret what we see, select the most workable of the multiple choices."

FURTHER READING

Slouching Towards Bethlehem (1968)

Play It as It Lays (1970)

The White Album (1979)

The Year of Magical Thinking (2005)

Blue Nights (2011)

JUDY BLUME

b. 1938

—◆◆◆◆—

I s there a tween girl in America who hasn't read *Are You There God? It's Me, Margaret*? Or who didn't secretly pass *Forever* around the classroom, hiding it under her mattress reading the turned-down pages when her parents weren't around? Without Judy Blume's guidance, how would any of us have gotten through all the embarrassments, challenges, and confusion of puberty? She says herself that when she was twelve years old, she wanted to learn about her growing breasts and getting her period and had nowhere to turn. As an adult she wrote the book she wished she'd had at the time. She taught generations of young people not to be ashamed of their bodies or emotions during adolescence, whether dealing with body image, female friendship, bullying, freckles, masturbation, sexuality, divorce, scoliosis, or substance abuse. She became the older, compassionate friend we all wish we had.

Blume grew up in Elizabeth, New Jersey, in the 1950s, the daughter of a dentist and a homemaker. In a culture that didn't discuss sex, or did so only in code ("be a good girl" or "don't get in trouble"), she was a self-described "Little Miss Perfect." She had a lot of questions and nowhere to turn, like so many of her peers. The contradiction between her efforts to appear perfect and the realities she observed in herself and the adults around her caused a lot of anxiety, which expressed itself in physical form with stomach problems and eczema. Blume was so bored with the books available for teenage girls that she would sometimes make up books to write her school book reports about.

Blume had had what she called a "secret life" from the time she was a young girl, constantly making up stories in her head about the things happening around her, just the ordinary day-to-day things or what adults around her were doing. When she got older, she kept what she called her "security notebook," where she would jot down her observations and ideas.

While a junior at NYU, she got married, and she was pregnant soon after. She became a suburban wife and mom with two small kids, which is what she was raised to believe was the right thing to do. But she was unhappy in her marriage, lonely, and frustrated. By age twenty-five, she felt that her life was over. The year she started writing, she had spent almost a year in bed with a variety of illnesses and ailments. She says that writing saved her. She went back and remembered the feelings she'd had as a young girl and started writing about them.

> I was a fearful child and can sometimes be a fearful adult, but I'm still fearless in my writing, so I know there's that other person inside me.

In fact, her first novel for grown-ups, *Wifey*, drew on that time. The protagonist tries to escape her boredom through sexual fantasies and an affair with an old boyfriend. When the book came out, there was concern it would be too shocking to her audience and end her career. It wasn't—the book sold well over four million copies.

Over more than five decades, Blume has written books for children of all ages, teenagers, and adults. Together they have sold more than eighty-five million copies and been translated into thirty-two languages. She has won more than ninety awards, including the National Book Foundation Medal for Distinguished Contribution to American Letters in 2004 and the Library of Congress's Living Legends award in 2000. She receives more than two thousand letters a month from children who view her as a friend, a safe person with whom they can share their fears, concerns, and questions. She published a collection of these letters, *Letters to Judy: What Kids Wish They Could Tell You*. In 2007, twenty-four female writers wrote an anthology of personal essays, reflecting on her influence in their lives: *Everything I Need to Know About Being a Girl I Learned from Judy Blume*.

Despite her popularity, since the 1980s her books have consistently appeared on the American Library Association's list of banned books more than any other author, particularly *Are You There God? It's Me, Margaret.* (which discusses menstruation and a desire to grow breasts), *Tiger Eyes* (which includes some mild sexuality, religious debates, and underage drinking and depicts teenage depression); *Blubber* (for descriptions of bullying and a couple of swear words), *Forever* (which shows healthy teenage sexuality with no bad consequences), and *Deenie* (yes, girls masturbate too). Judy felt that "I had to write the most honest books I could. It never occurred to me, at the time, that what I was writing was controversial. Much of it grew out of my own feelings and concerns when I was young."

Blume's feeling is that kids are going to hear about it or live through it one way or the other, and it's better to read about it in all its complexity in a way that is ultimately positive, not shaming. They will skip over the parts they aren't ready for yet and will ask questions about the parts they don't understand.

Blume is a champion for free speech and intellectual freedom and works diligently with the National Coalition Against Censorship. While some people would still prefer to keep some aspects of life secret, a writer's job is clearly to speak the unspoken, to be an advocate for honesty.

✦✦✦✦✦✦✦✦✦✦✦✦✦

FURTHER READING

Are You There God? It's Me, Margaret. (1970)

Tales of a Fourth Grade Nothing (1972)

Deenie (1973)

Forever (1975)

Wifey (1978)

✦✦✦✦✦✦✦✦✦✦✦✦✦

MARGARET ATWOOD

b. 1939

———◆◆◆◆———

Margaret Atwood doesn't want you calling her a feminist. If you are going to, she asks that you please define what you mean by the term first. As far as she is concerned, women's rights are human rights. And she is interested in human rights and examining the human condition, with all its power struggles, inequities, failures, and triumphs.

Atwood's thesis at Harvard was on the Victorian, or social, novel, and her interest in examining society continues in her work today. She has written about male-female relationships, male brutality in a patriarchal society, the status of women, the use and abuse of power, climate change and human extinction, designer humans, female sexuality, Canada's struggle to create an identity in the context of the American Empire, and, in recent years, human rights. Much of what she writes about may seem like postapocalyptic fantasy (or nightmare, really), but things like the mandatory motherhood and controlling of women's bodies in *The Handmaid's Tale* echo reality for too many women. Atwood says that men often ask her why her female characters are so paranoid. Her response: "It's not paranoia. It's recognition of their situation." Atwood seems able to recognize and articulate tragic flaws in society before the rest of us.

She spent her childhood in Northern Ontario with her parents and brother, in almost total isolation at an insect research station in a log cabin her father helped build, running through the wilderness in pants, collecting bugs in jars, and learning the ways of nature. Treated as an equal to her brother, she was homeschooled by her scientist father and nutritionist mother, who collected their curriculum, workbooks, and reading material such as *Grimm's Fairy Tales* by mail order. Atwood didn't spend an entire year in a traditional school until she was eleven. She began to write poetry in high school and, at sixteen, committed herself to a writing career, publishing a collection of poems, *Double Persephone*, six years later. Her second book of poetry, *The Circle Game*, earned her Canada's highest literary honor, the Governor General's Award. At the University of Toronto, she started studying philosophy before changing to literature. She attended Harvard for her master's and received a fellowship but then dropped out to pursue her writing.

The barriers to women writing are often in place
at a very early age and in very basic ways.

————

The Handmaid's Tale, to give a most simplistic description, is about fertile women in a society where they are rare and stripped of the ability to earn money, own property, or read and write and are forced to reproduce for powerful, barren couples. This chilling dystopian narrative struck a chord in a society continually grappling with parallel issues and has not been out of print since it was first published in 1985, selling several million copies worldwide, with countless translations and editions. It has been adapted into a popular film and TV series and has become something of a catchphrase ("It's like something out of *The Handmaid's Tale*" or "Make Margaret Atwood fiction again") and a symbol for protestors of policies controlling women's bodies, with groups dressed in the handmaids' familiar red cloak and white bonnets gathering in front of state and federal legislatures.

Atwood had three interests that came together in her writing: her fascination with dystopian literature from Aldous Huxley, George Orwell, and Ray Bradbury; her studies at Harvard of seventeenth- and eighteenth-century history and literature in America (one of her ancestors was "half hanged Mary," a seventeenth-century woman accused of witchcraft in Massachusetts); and her interest in military history and "dictatorships and how they function." She said that when she sat down to write *The Handmaid's Tale* she had two rules for herself: "I would not include anything that human beings had not already done in some other place or time, or for which the technology did not already exist." She is a compulsive collector of research and newspaper clippings, and her book's title came from an Associated Press article about a Catholic congregation in New Jersey taken over by fundamentalists, where wives were called "handmaidens." The state-sanctioned rape is pulled straight from the Old Testament. In other words, don't blame her for her story; she did her homework, and it has all been done before.

Atwood wrote the book while living in West Berlin, and the experience took its toll on her. Her literary agent saw her during the writing and said she looked like hell and asked her what happened. "It's the new novel. It scares me. But I have to write it." She was mostly afraid of the bleak future she describes, but also confesses to having the fears that most writers eventually, inevitably have: "I lose my nerve, or think instead of the horrors of publication and what I will be accused of in reviews." When the book was published, Atwood's daughter was nine years old, and by the time she was in high school a few years later, despite some dismissive reviews, it had become required reading.

The much-anticipated sequel to *Handmaid's Tale*, *The Testaments*, was released in the fall of 2019 and broke sales records immediately in the United States and Canada, receiving glowing reviews.

Atwood travels often and can write anywhere: on a plane, on a borrowed typewriter in the woods, on hotel stationery, or even on her hand if necessary. Her flexibility and versatility are astonishing. She has a million and a half Twitter followers and has innovated remote book signings with LongPen. Her experimentation with and embrace of technology stem from her belief that it is actually good for literacy; after all, if you can't read, you can't tweet or read fanfiction on Wattpad.

In *Negotiating with the Dead*, Atwood explores the motives of other writers and herself, as the author of more than forty books. After a long list of entertaining, witty, and oh-too-familiar reasons (to impress girls, to change the cultural consciousness), she comes to the conclusion that "possibly, then, writing has to do with darkness, and a desire or perhaps a compulsion to enter it and with luck, to illuminate it, and to bring something back out to the light."

◆ ◆ ◆ ◆ ◆ ◆ ◆ ◆ ◆ ◆ ◆ ◆ ◆ ◆

FURTHER READING

The Handmaid's Tale (1985)

Alias Grace (1996)

The Blind Assassin (2000)

The Robber Bride (2003)

Oryx and Crake (2003)

The Year of the Flood (2009)

The Testaments (2019)

Negotiating with the Dead (2002)

◆ ◆ ◆ ◆ ◆ ◆ ◆ ◆ ◆ ◆ ◆ ◆ ◆ ◆

OCTAVIA BUTLER

1947–2006

———◆◆◆◆———

I began writing about power because I had so little.

———

A s a child her aunt told her, "Honey, Negroes can't be writers," but she still begged her mother for a Remington typewriter and started recording her stories. Octavia Butler says she was inspired to write science fiction when she was twelve, after watching what she called "a terrible movie," *Devil Girl from Mars*, about a bunch of "man-hungry" Martian women. She thought to herself, "Geez, I can write a better story than that." She started devouring science fiction magazines and submitting her stories to them. When she was growing up during the race to space between the United States and the U.S.S.R., astronauts were heroes and education in science was being supported, which helped form her deeply realistic and researched writing style.

As a trailblazer in a genre dominated by white men, Butler asked the question, "Why aren't there more Science Fiction Black writers? What we don't see, we assume can't be. What a destructive assumption." Ahead of her time, she started writing in the 1970s, and the rest of the world is just now starting to catch up with her. Butler has influenced countless artists of all kinds. Hilton Als has identified her as the "dominant artistic force" throughout Beyoncé's film version of *Lemonade*, and Ava DuVernay is adapting *Dawn*, one of Butler's Xenogenesis novels, for television. Janelle Monáe said that Butler was a direct influence for her album *The ArchAndroid*.

Octavia Estelle Butler was born in Pasadena, California; her father shined shoes and her mother was a housekeeper. She was extremely tall and socially awkward and had dyslexia. She graduated from Pasadena City College and went on to the Screen Writers Guild Open Door Program and the Clarion Science Fiction and Fantasy Writers' Workshop, where novelist Harlan Ellison became a mentor. She had jobs as a secretary and as an assembly line worker in a factory while she worked on her writing, eventually being able to support herself full-time with it when she published the novel *Kindred*.

As the author of twelve novels and numerous short stories, Butler was the first science fiction writer to receive a MacArthur Genius Fellowship.

Her work transcended the conventions of the genre and shone a light on many social issues. She used time travel, parallel universes, alien battles, hybrid species, and shapeshifting characters to write about contemporary issues: environmental and economic crisis, global warming, drug addiction, technology, communication, prejudice and class conflict almost causing the destruction of the world, alienation and transcendence, violence and spirituality, slavery and freedom, separation and community.

She has been called a predictor of the future because her books discussed the repercussions of climate change well before it became part of the collective consciousness, and many of her themes portend the current political climate (one of her characters, a presidential candidate, appealed to the religious right with the slogan "Help Us to Make America Great Again" in 1998!). She said her books are not prophecies as much as cautionary tales. These science fiction fables—she called several of them parables—discussed racism and misogyny and patriarchy with a refreshing bluntness, all couched within a rich understanding of spirituality, mysticism, and mythology.

Butler built worlds for the disenfranchised as a way to express the importance of humans connecting and sticking together, despite cultural or social differences. And even if her characters were sometimes shapeshifting aliens or covered in tentacles, at the core of her work, she was always exploring the universal question: *What does it mean to be human?*

◆◆◆◆◆◆◆◆◆◆◆◆◆◆

FURTHER READING

Kindred (1979)

Patternists series:

Wild Seed (1980), *Mind of My Mind* (1977), *Clay's Ark* (1984), *Survivor* (1978), *Patternmaster* (1976)

Xenogenesis series:

Dawn (1987), *Adulthood Rites* (1988), *Imago* (1989)

Earthseed series:

Parable of the Sower (1993), *Parable of the Talents* (1998)

◆◆◆◆◆◆◆◆◆◆◆◆◆◆

JEANETTE WINTERSON

b. 1959

——— ◆◆◆◆ ———

G rowing up working-class in England, Jeanette Winterson's Pentecostal mother gardened and felt that the vegetables were either "godly" or "ungodly." Jerusalem artichokes were good. Leeks, being phallic, were bad. Jeanette always loved to be close to nature, godly or un-, and today grows a lot of her own food and breeds sheep. As soon as she started making money from her work, she bought an old building and turned it into Verde's, a fruit and vegetable market in London's East End. She doesn't say whether the fruits or vegetables have moral characteristics, but they are delicious. And fruit plays a big part in her writing.

> I still have that rather magical sense about books—
> that they do, somehow, have special powers.

———

In 1985, Winterson published the fictionalized autobiography *Oranges Are Not the Only Fruit*, about a young lesbian trying to find herself and how she fits in. It launched her writing career and became one of the first mainstream novels about gay women. But even though the protagonist is called Jeanette, and the experiences mirror those in her own life, she once explained, "The question put to the writer 'How much of this is based on your own experience?' is meaningless. All or nothing may be the answer." In the same vein, she does not like being called a "lesbian writer" because it limits the value of her work to that one quality. She writes about love, passion, and the "agony of intimacy," which are universal.

When she started out as a writer, the odds were stacked against her. Winterson was young, female, working-class, and gay. She had also been adopted and had a complicated childhood—her father was a factory worker, and her mother took her

out of school regularly to travel to gospel revivals. Winterson created her own philosophical outlook and experimental narrative form that eliminates some of the usual details and characteristics that create an identity. As someone who has dealt with the prejudices of class, gender, and sexual orientation, she prefers that her readers "identify with a being, with a state of consciousness," rather than a character with all sorts of preconceived notions placed on them because of who they appear to be on the outside. In her first breakout book in the United States, *Written on the Body*, the voice of the narrator has no gender, name, or age and goes by the pronoun "they." This was in 1992.

Jeanette's birth mother was a teenage factory worker in Manchester, England, who couldn't support a child. Jack and Constance Winterson adopted her and raised her in revival tents and church, hoping she would become a missionary and save people's souls. She was raised on literal readings of the Bible and the belief that the Apocalypse was coming. She preached on street corners as a child. When she disappointed her mother, she would be told, "The Devil led us to the wrong crib." There were no books allowed in the house other than the Bible and religious texts, because, as Jeanette says, "My mother knew that sedition and controversy are fired by printed matter. It was because she knew the power of books that she avoided them." Somehow a copy of *Morte d'Arthur*—the classic telling of King Arthur and his Knights of the Round Table— slipped through, and it had a deep influence on Jeanette. She started sneaking books into the house, hiding them under her mattress. As her bed rose higher and higher, her mother finally took notice and, after pulling out D. H. Lawrence, confiscated all the books and burned them in the backyard. But what Jeanette had read in those books stayed with her.

At sixteen, she fell in love with another girl and was thrown out of the house. When her mother asked her why she would continue this forbidden relationship, even knowing she would become homeless, Jeanette said, "She makes me happy." Her mother responded with "Why be happy when you could be normal?" which became the title of Winterson's 2011 memoir, which she wrote when a breakup triggered all of her unresolved childhood issues and provoked a midlife mental health crisis and a suicide attempt.

She started working—selling ice cream, cleaning in a mental hospital, and serving as an undertaker's assistant—to put herself through Oxford University. When *Oranges Are Not the Only Fruit* came out, it won the Whitbread First Novel award, and that, combined with word of mouth, ignited its critical and commercial success. Winterson followed it with *The Passion*, a magical realism fable with a bisexual heroine; *Sexing the Cherry*, which intertwines several fairy tales across time and space; and the beautiful, poetic, and erotic—you can't call it a "tale" exactly, more like an ode or celebration—of mad, passionate love and its loss, *Written on the Body*. All were bold, imaginative, and strikingly original, and each publication grew her readership.

What some people viewed as her arrogance after her early success, as well as her combative attitude and evangelical fervor, has made her a controversial figure. She has dealt with a lot of hostility simply for being who she is and because of her experimental narrative forms, which have changed the novel but have not always been well received by critics or the literary establishment. If she has a chip on her shoulder, she has probably earned it. But it is the readers who matter to her, as well as the writers who have followed her: "There was so much misogyny, homophobia, anti-working class stuff . . . other women came before me and made things possible for me. Every time a new generation comes along, we open the space a bit more."

Hallelujah.

✦✦✦✦✦✦✦✦✦✦✦✦✦✦

FURTHER READING

Oranges Are Not the Only Fruit (1985)

Sexing the Cherry (1989)

Written on the Body (1992)

Frankissstein (2019)

✦✦✦✦✦✦✦✦✦✦✦✦✦✦

Where There's a Wand, There's a Way
J. K. ROWLING
b. 1965

—◆◆◆◆—

I t's difficult to imagine the time before *Hogwarts*, *Butterbeer*, *dementors*, and *Quidditch* entered our common lexicon. Joanne Rowling, in addition to being the great imagination behind those creations, also has the unique distinction of being the first writer—male or female—to become a billionaire through her work (although her estimated worth is now closer to $650 million because of the large amount of money she has given to charities). She wanted to make her mark on the world as a writer from a young age. To say she did just that would be a major understatement. She influenced a generation with her Harry Potter franchise and is credited with reviving children's book publishing in the early twenty-first century.

Rowling grew up along the border of England and Wales; her father was an aircraft engineer and her mother a science technician. Jo always knew she would be a writer and wrote her first story when she was six, about a rabbit with the measles. She wrote her first novel, about seven cursed diamonds and their owners, when she was eleven. She says she lived for books and was your garden-variety bookworm who was perfectly happy alone in a room either reading or making up stories. She said her teenage years were awful, in part because her mother was diagnosed with multiple sclerosis. She died before any of the Harry Potter books were published.

After graduating from the University of Exeter with a degree in French, Rowling worked at Amnesty International and then taught English in Portugal, where she got married, had a baby (named Jessica in honor of one of her favorite writers, Jessica Mitford), and started jotting down her notes. When the marriage ended in a difficult divorce—and while Joanne suffered from clinical depression—she moved to Edinburgh with her daughter and a suitcase containing the first three chapters of what would become *Harry Potter and the Philosopher's Stone*. While her daughter napped, she would sit in a café and work on the book, all while living on state benefits. She would later say in a commencement speech given at Harvard University that at

that time she was "jobless, a lone parent, and as poor as it is possible to be in modern Britain, without being homeless . . . By every usual standard, I was the biggest failure I knew."

She first came up with the idea for her characters Harry, Hermione, and Ron when she was stuck on a delayed train for four hours. She began writing down her thoughts and characters and mapped out all seven books in the series over the course of the next five years. When she finished the first book, *Harry Potter and the Philosopher's Stone*, it was rejected by twelve major publishing houses; it took a year for her agent to place the book with Bloomsbury, for a very small advance, after the editor's eight-year-old daughter fell in love with the first chapter. It became so successful that an American publisher, Scholastic, picked it up, changing the title to *Harry Potter and the Sorcerer's Stone*. Eventually the film rights to the book were sold for seven figures, and from there the books became the hottest publishing property all over the world. When the sixth book, *The Half-Blood Prince*, was released, it sold nine million copies in the first twenty-four hours.

> Imagination is not only the uniquely human capacity to envision that which is not, and therefore the fount of all invention and innovation. In its arguably most transformative and revelatory capacity, it is the power to that enables us to empathize with humans whose experiences we have never shared.

———

The phenomenon became the catalyst for tens of thousands of pieces of fan-fiction, several companion volumes, and the launch of Rowling's digital company, Pottermore. The world that she created came to life beyond the movies with the Wizarding World of Harry Potter theme park at Universal Studios, which re-created Hogwarts Castle, the village of Hogsmeade, and the Forbidden Forest, complete with fire-breathing dragons, magic shops, and Butterbeer ice cream.

Over the years, some religious groups and individuals in various countries have banned or even burned her books, calling them sacrilegious or claiming they promote Satanism. Hogwash. They object to the magic, even though Harry uses it to battle evil. It sounds a bit like burning a witch at the stake, no?

But of course, no matter how many people burn the books, they can't take them out of the cultural imagination.

Rowling has continued to make her voice heard in her post-Potter years. In addition to contributing to spinoffs set in the Harry Potter universe, including a Broadway play and a series of *Fantastic Beasts* movies, she has written crime fiction for adults under a pseudonym and a new novel for younger children. She has also waded into controversy at times. In the heated political environment ahead of the vote on Scottish independence from the UK in 2014, she was a vocal opponent of the referendum and at one point became the largest donor to the anti-independence Better Together campaign. And more recently, she has become a polarizing figure in the debate about rights for transgender people in the UK and beyond, making statements online that many, including some of the stars of the Harry Potter movies, have criticized as anti-trans.

Without a doubt, Rowling's influence has gone beyond her readers: she has impacted the entire culture and almost single-handedly revived the market for fantasy and young adult novels. And regardless of where her pen takes her next, she has inspired countless other writers and introduced a generation of readers to the magic of books.

FURTHER READING

Harry Potter and the Sorcerer's Stone (1997) aka *Harry Potter and the Philosopher's Stone*

Harry Potter and the Chamber of Secrets (1998)

Harry Potter and the Prisoner of Azkaban (1999)

Harry Potter and the Goblet of Fire (2000)

Harry Potter and the Order of the Phoenix (2001)

Harry Potter and the Half-Blood Prince (2005)

Harry Potter and the Deathly Hallows (2007)

Harry Potter and the Cursed Child, Parts I & II (2016)

Fantastic Beasts and Where to Find Them (2001)

The Casual Vacancy (2012)

JHUMPA LAHIRI

b. 1967

◆◆◆◆

When I write, when I try to write, I always feel uncomfortable.
You need to dig where you don't feel comfortable.

―――――

Jhumpa Lahiri takes language very seriously. When she was a child in Rhode Island, whenever she went shopping with her parents, the salesperson would always speak first to her, assuming that her parents didn't speak English, even though they were fluent, a teacher and university librarian. She spoke Bengali at home, but she didn't read or write it. The books of her childhood were distinctly American or British: Laura Ingalls Wilder, *The Lion, the Witch and the Wardrobe*. At school she had a group of friends who would sit at recess and make up stories together. She admits to stealing blank notebooks from her teacher's cabinet in order to write those stories down. Despite the fact that her family had moved to the United States when she was a toddler, Jhumpa was made fun of for the things that made her different, and people made assumptions about her because her parents were Indian.

Lahiri studied and excelled at Latin, and she calls Ovid's *The Metamorphoses* one of the most influential books of her life.

Like many second-generation Americans, Lahiri says, "When I was growing up . . . I felt neither Indian nor American . . . I felt intense pressure to be two things, loyal to the old world and fluent in the new." Her writing reflects her "desire to force the two worlds I occupied to mingle on the page," with all the loneliness, rootlessness, and alienation that go with this dual identity.

She visited Calcutta, her parents' hometown, many times as a child and adult and learned from her relatives, who were visual artists, that the life of an artist is a precarious one. But she felt compelled to write, and as she got older she did so as a way to connect with her parents, wanting to show them that she understood the world that they came from. And she says that when she became a writer, her desk became her true home.

Lahiri's academic pedigree is top-notch: undergrad at Barnard, an M.A. and Ph.D. from Boston University, teaching at Princeton and elsewhere. Like most writers, when she first started sending work to magazines, she was rejected, but many of her stories were eventually (during her twenties!) published in the *New Yorker*.

Her debut book, *Interpreter of Maladies*, a collection of stories published in 1999, won the Pulitzer Prize for fiction. In fact, she has won so many awards for her writing (the National Humanities Medal, the O. Henry Prize, the PEN/Hemingway Award . . . really, the list goes on and on). To date, she has written three more successful books, including the popular *The Namesake*, which was made into a film in 2004.

Really, when you win a Pulitzer at thirty-two, where is there to go? Lahiri refuses to be limited by her subject matter and background. To her, writing is freedom, and she doesn't want others' expectations forced upon her. She may have opened the door for other writers who are the children of immigrants, but she publicly wonders why the focus is so much on her cultural background, instead of the aesthetics of her writing.

Lahiri's conflicts regarding identity led her to create a broader one. She fell in love with the Italian language, spent years learning it, moved to Rome, and started writing in Italian. Her *In Other Words* was written in Italian (and translated into English by the same woman who translated Elena Ferrante), and she also edited a collection of Italian short stories, published in English for the first time, many of which she translated herself from Italian into English.

When she moved to Rome with her husband and two children, they had to learn to navigate the basics of everyday life: how to get around by bus or subway, how to make friends, how to open the front door to her apartment. In her bewilderment she started writing in a notebook and thinking in Italian for the first time: "As a writer I can demolish myself. I can reconstruct myself." She underwent her own, self-inflicted metamorphosis.

FURTHER READING

Interpreter of Maladies (1999)

The Namesake (2003)

Unaccustomed Earth (2008)

The Lowland (2013)

In Other Words (2015)

CHIMAMANDA NGOZI ADICHIE

b. 1977

◆◆◆◆

Stories have been used to dispossess and to malign.
But stories can also be used to empower, and to humanize.

———

Chimamanda Ngozi Adichie calls herself a "happy African feminist who does not hate men." She was once asked by a journalist not to call herself a feminist because "those are women who are unhappy because they can't find husbands." She is quite happily married to a handsome doctor and has a young daughter, thank you very much. She is also an internationally famous public intellectual, a bestselling author of novels, short stories, and essays, who has been translated into thirty languages, and the winner of multiple literary awards and a MacArthur Foundation Award, and was the 2018 commencement speaker at Harvard University. Her work is required reading at schools all over the world.

She also is known for her love of lip gloss, high heels, and high fashion; she inspired the Christian Dior T-shirt and handbag with the name of her famous TED Talk and essay "We Should All Be Feminists" written across them. Beyoncé sampled her words in a song and music video. She became the face of Boots No. 7 makeup.

Adichie started writing when she was around seven or, as she says, as soon as she could spell, claiming, "I didn't choose writing, writing chose me. This may sound slightly mythical, but I sometimes feel as if my writing is something bigger than I am." She was the fifth of six children in an upper-middle-class, tight-knit, Catholic family. Her father was a professor and her mother an administrator at the University of Nigeria. Although she did spend one year at medical school to satisfy her high-achieving family, she ultimately chose the uncertain life of a writer, publishing her first book of poems when she was nineteen. Her debut novel, *Purple Hibiscus*, was initially rejected by many agents and publishers in the United States because "nobody cared about Nigeria," she's said.

Growing up under the uncertainty of military dictatorships and in the shadow of war was difficult, but Adichie is proud of her Nigerian heritage. In *Americanah*, she looks at the differences between African immigrants to the United States and African Americans. She says she did not know she was black until she moved to America and came to understand its fraught feelings about race. She writes about the value of the differences between people and our shared humanity. She is here to take our assumptions about race, gender, class, and culture and turn them upside down, to make us see others with more open eyes.

Adichie is courageous in using her words and encourages others to be the same. Her writing is so direct and seemingly straightforward it makes the impact of her words inescapable. She chooses them carefully and wisely, without florid embellishment. She is crystal clear in ways that surprise people. She knows the importance of speaking and writing the truth, providing clarity in a world gone mad with warped perceptions and distortions of fact. She knows that the stories we tell—the ones we tell ourselves and the ones we tell the world—shape who we are as individuals and as a society.

Of course, using words in such a responsible and thoughtful way does not come without struggle. Writing about her experiences has been painful; she has suffered from depression and self-doubt. She also knows that you cannot create anything of value without both self-doubt *and* self-belief. Chimamanda means "my personal spirit will never be broken." You can say that again. She knows that words, expressed as clear, well-thought-out ideas, not just as manipulations, have incredible power. They have power to change the world. Adichie has, indeed, done just that with hers.

FURTHER READING

Purple Hibiscus (2003)

Half of a Yellow Sun (2006)

The Thing Around Your Neck (2009)

Americanah (2013)

We Should All Be Feminists (2014)

Dear Ijeawele, or A Feminist Manifesto in Fifteen Suggestions (2017)

A NOTE ON SOURCES

I am by no means a scholar or literary critic, so I depended a tremendous amount on the work of people who are. In studying and learning about these brave broads, I read countless articles, websites, books, reviews, interviews, and interpretations—to say nothing of reading a good chunk (or at least a strong sampling) of the work of each of the women profiled. As a result, I have consulted well over four hundred sources. Here, in the name of time and space, I am mentioning just some of the invaluable books and periodicals I turned to again and again. If you want to go down the rabbit hole with me, a complete list of sources can be found on my website: www.laurenmarinobooks.com.

In many cases there are websites devoted to these women, whether they are official sites created by the author or her estate, or various fan sites or societies. If you are interested in a particular writer, there is probably a website devoted to her, and within that website there will be not only a wealth of information but also links to more pages, events, works, and information. Here is a smattering:

www.janeausten.org

www.bronte.org.uk

www.virginiawoolfblog.com

www.virginiawoolfsociety.org.uk

www.judyblume.com

www.margaretatwood.ca

www.ursulakleguin.com

www.tonimorrisonsociety.org

www.jkrowling.com

www.rachelcarson.org

www.louisamayalcott.org

www.thejoandidion.com

www.mayaangelou.com

www.chimamanda.com

If you are looking to dig deeper into the life and works of the women profiled in this book—or explore many more whom I couldn't include—I refer you to the following general interest (more or less) works. Specific biographies are listed either in the "Further Reading" section of each entry or on my website (Hermione Lee on Virginia Woolf and Edith Wharton, Judith Thurman on Colette, Claire Harmon on Charlotte Brontë, Jane Todd on Aphra Behn, etc.).

Passionate Minds: Women Rewriting the World, by Claudia Roth Pierpont. Alfred A. Knopf, 2000.

The Literary Ladies' Guide to the Writing Life: Inspiration and Advice from Celebrated Women Authors Who Paved the Way, by Nava Atlas. Sellers Publishing, 2000.

The Norton Anthology of Literature by Women: The Traditions in English, volume 1, third edition, by Sandra M. Gilbert and Susan Gubar (editors). In addition to well-selected writing by the women profiled here, the introductions by Gilbert and Gubar were invaluable in creating context.

A Jury of Her Peers: Celebrating American Women Writers from Anne Bradstreet to Annie Proulx, by Elaine Showalter. Vintage, 2010.

The Vintage Book of American Women Writers, by Elaine Showalter. Vintage, 2011.

A Literature of Their Own: British Novelists from Brontë to Lessing, expanded edition, by Elaine Showalter. Princeton University Press, 1998.

Expanding the Canon of Early Modern Women's Writing, by Paul Salzman (author and editor). Cambridge Scholars Publishing, 2010.

A Secret Sisterhood: The Literary Friendships of Jane Austen, Charlotte Brontë, George Eliot, and Virginia Woolf, by Emily Midorikawa and Emma Claire Sweeney. Mariner Books, 2017.

The Madwoman in the Attic: The Woman Writer and the Nineteenth-Century Literary Imagination, by Sandra M. Gilbert and Susan Gubar, Yale University Press, originally published in 1979. This is a groundbreaking classic of feminist literary theory, reissued in a second edition in 2000.

Other sources I found myself turning to again and again were the *Paris Review* interviews with authors; Maria Popova's Brain Pickings blog; many, many articles in the *New Yorker, Literary Hub,* the *New York Times*, and the *Guardian*; the Poetry Foundation; and PBS's American Masters series of documentary biographies.